Please renew/return this item by the last date shown.

So that your telephone call is charged at local rate, please call the numbers as set out below:

	From Area codes 01923 or 0208:	From the rest of Herts:
Renewals:	01923 471373	01438 737373
Enquiries:	01923 471333	01438 737333
Minicom:	01923 471599	01438 737599

L32b

5 MAR 2008

Please renew/retur... ...own.
Thank yo...
Hertfordshire ... ...on
L32

D1332988

The
Recipes
of
Hannah Woolley

*English Cookery
of the Seventeenth Century*

THE
RECIPES
of
Hannah Woolley

ENGLISH
COOKERY
of the
Seventeenth Century

Edited For Today's Cooks
and Introduced by

MATTHEW HAMLYN

Heinemann Kingswood

Heinemann Kingswood
Michelin House, 81 Fulham Road, London SW3 6RB
LONDON MELBOURNE AUCKLAND

Copyright © 1988 Matthew Hamlyn

First published 1988

ISBN 0 434 98102 8

Photoset by Deltatype Ltd, Ellesmere Port
Printed and bound in Great Britain by
Richard Clay Ltd, Bungay, Suffolk

Designed by Geoff Green

In memory of my father,
who helped me to realise the true value
of good food, good wine, and good company.

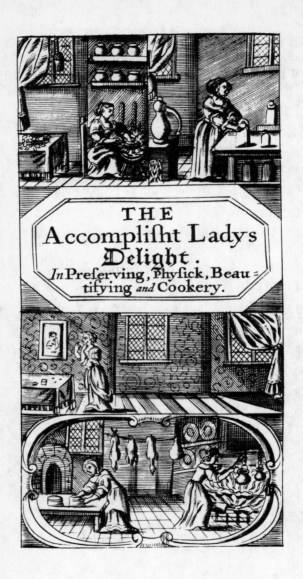

The title page from
The Accomplisht-Ladys Delight
which is attributed to
Hannah Woolley. Published in 1675.

CONTENTS

INTRODUCTION

IT TAKES a certain amount of courage, even in these enlightened days, to attempt the compilation of a book of English recipes. The British race, while happy to boast of its superiority in most areas of human endeavour, tends to shy away from culinary excellence. It is only comparatively recently, for instance, that English head chefs have been appointed to run the great restaurant and hotel kitchens. Despite (at last) a growing interest in a specifically British way of cooking, the fashion for all things French (look at most expensive menus) is still widespread, and it is almost *de rigeur* for sophisticated diners-out to lump together English food along with English weather and licensing laws, as reasons for despising the place, and spending one's holidays in gastronomic pilgrimages round Tuscany or the Perigord.

Native dislike for the food produced in this country is not, however, a modern development. The nineteenth century seems to have produced both a decline in good English cooking and a natural reaction against it. Instead of trying to improve traditional food, the discerning eater turned his attention across the Channel, and buried his memories of soggy cabbage and greyish roast beef under the exotic sauces and culinary *legerdemain* of great French chefs such as Antonin Carême, who was imported by the Prince Regent to run the kitchens of the Brighton Pavilion, and Alexis Soyer, who was the first chef of the Reform Club, and who spent virtually all his working life here. A dichotomy was established of the French *grande cuisine*, produced by male chefs on the one hand, and plain English cooking, produced by female cooks, on the other. Of the latter, the pseudonymous author of *Dinners and Dishes* (1885), caustically wrote, in a chapter entitled 'British Atrocities':

there are twenty ways of cooking potatoes, of which three only are known in England, and one alone, that of boiling, extensively practised.

And Oscar Wilde, reviewing the same book, describes the typical British cook in strong language:

> Her entire ignorance of herbs, her passion for extracts and essences, her total inability to make a soup which is anything more than a combination of pepper and gravy . . . the British cook is a foolish woman, who should be turned, for her iniquities, into a pillar of that salt which she never knows how to use.

Some of these sins are still around today, and perhaps the passion for extracts and essences is even more pronounced. Decent food has been revived in Britain, to rescue a public tired both of dismal British food and the worst excesses of the French tradition, but this revival, once again, has been essentially a foreign influence, tied in with the greater availability of fresh exotic produce and more foreign travel, rather than a revival of indigenous cooking.

Recently, there has been a new interest in real English food, the cooking of the period before the nineteenth century, when so much seemed to go wrong. People are beginning to realise that English food has not always been roasted and boiled, and that the dullness of 'English food' is a product of watering down old traditions or unsuccessfully attempting to copy new foreign ones. I became interested in the subject while exploring different aspects of cooking. Having been brought up by Elizabeth David-trained parents I had a good grounding in the standard French and Italian cuisine, to which I added experiments in Russian, East European and (typically of most students who can actually hold a saucepan, I suppose) Indian cooking. But the revelation of English food, specifically that of the seventeenth century, came about almost by accident. I had been asked to teach some undergraduates about Alexander Pope and, while hastily refreshing my memory about him, I came across a small volume of essays by the late John Butt, a distinguished literary critic and scholar. Most of them were about Pope, but there was also an address, originally given to the Buckingham Mothers Union in 1931, called 'The Domestic Manuals of Hannah Wolley [sic]'. I was intrigued by his excerpts from her writings, and set to work to discover more of them in the Bodleian Library in Oxford.

Firstly, I found her recipes historically interesting, simply because I had never given much thought to what sort of food people ate at that time, and the conditions under which it was prepared. But

I also found them attractive, and decided that some of them might well be worth trying out on my family and friends. When they in turn told me that the dishes were not only 'interesting' but delicious, I began to think of putting some of them together in a modernised form for a wider range of people to enjoy. The present selection of recipes is the fruit of many highly entertaining, and occasionally frustrating, hours of experiment in my kitchen, which, incidentally, is far removed from the gleaming, superbly equipped working places associated with more exalted practitioners. I can honestly say that, if these dishes can be prepared in my small, slightly lopsided kitchen, they can be made anywhere with a sharp knife, a blender and a reasonably decent cooker.

Interest in the recipes led me to Mrs Woolley's other work, which covers a remarkable range of subjects, all useful for the better instruction of the female sex, 'from *Childhood* down to *Old-age*'. Her writing career started with a book on preserving fruit, and continued in successive volumes through medicine, letter-writing, deportment and so on. In the process of instruction, she gives the modern reader a vivid picture of the society in which she lived, and which was the setting for the dishes I've attempted to reproduce. For this reason alone I thought it worthwhile to include a selection from these writings in the present volume, but they also give a flavour of the sort of woman she was. Her work has a strong autobiographical streak, and it is possible to build up quite a detailed portrait of her character and career from it. It is rare to find any autobiography written by women in this period, and we are lucky that such a colourful and resourceful woman as Mrs Woolley decided to put pen to paper. She writes forcefully, and often amusingly, about herself and her work, and if the reader finds it all as interesting, and on occasion as amusing, as I did myself, I shall be well pleased.

I should like to acknowledge the help I have had from the marvellous and indispensable *Jane Grigson's Vegetable Book*, which is full of recondite information and profitable suggestions. Hilary Spurling's fascinating and extremely scholarly *Elinor Fettiplace's Receipt Book* appeared too late for me to make very much use of it, but I am grateful for some hints that I don't think I would have found elsewhere, as well as for the comforting feeling that I was not working wholly on my own in this field. No-one interested in the history of English food can fail to recognise the importance of Dorothy Hartley's *Food in England*, which is evocatively written and full of thought-provoking facts and suggestions. For information on Mrs Woolley's life and times, I used a wide variety of sources, among which I should mention *Before the Blue Stockings* by Asa Wallas, Antonia Fraser's *The Weaker Vessel* and Lawrence Stone's *The Family, Sex and Marriage in England 1500–1800*. However, the most important source of all was the book by John Butt, *Pope, Dickens and Others*, which first alerted me – entirely by chance – to the existence of Mrs Woolley. Finally, special thanks to my family and friends (especially those living in Crown St) who heroically ate their way through all that seventeenth century food and survived to make constructive com- ments and encouraging remarks. I hope the reader finds it as enjoyable to cook and eat as we all did.

THE LIFE, TIMES AND
WORKS OF HANNAH WOOLLEY

THE story of Hannah Woolley's life is interesting, firstly because Mrs Woolley was a remarkable character in her own right, whose career would probably have been worth studying in any age. Furthermore, because her writing is concerned with social life, with all the details of food and drink, clothes and manners, it provides a vivid insight into the society in which she lived. Best of all, from the historian's point of view, is the fact that she wrote a good deal of autobiography. Indeed, our main source of information about Hannah Woolley's life is her own work: scattered among her writings there are many autobiographical passages, which in a period when few women wrote at all, and even fewer wrote autobiography, are invaluable. Such self-portraits are usually inserted to emphasize her own abilities, and to show how they helped her triumph over the many vicissitudes with which she was afflicted. It is worth remembering, therefore, that her recollections are coloured by the need for commercial self-promotion. In the 'Short Account of the life and abilities of the Authoress of this book' prefixed to *The Gentlewoman's Companion*, she writes:

> I would not presume to trouble you with any passages of my life, or relate my innate qualifications, or acquired, were it not in obedience to a Person of Honour, who engag'd me so to do, for no other reason than to stop the mouths of such who may be so maliciously censorious as to believe I pretend what I cannot perform . . . Now to the intent I may increase your wonder, I shall relate how I came to the knowledge of what I profess.

In the face of such determined self-advertisement, perhaps just a little enhancement of her good points here and there may be assumed, but no more than one would find in the autobiographies of any self-made man or woman. There is certainly no reason to suppose that the story she tells is in essence anything other than true, and where independent historical records exist, they support her recollections. As Mrs Woolley's biography is so closely connected with her writings, and her life and works are so much a part of the times in which she lived, I shall tell her story with plenty of quotations from her books, and relate what she wrote to the social history of the period.

Few exact details are known about Mrs Woolley's birth and early years. She does not mention her maiden name, nor when or where, precisely, she was born. However, from various pieces of evidence, it seems clear she was born in about 1623, almost certainly in Essex. By her own account, she was something of a prodigy. Her mother and elder sisters were 'very well skilled in Physick and Chyrugery', and she learned a little from them about these and other subjects. It cannot have been that little, for, her parents dying 'when very young', she was able to start earning her living as a teacher, rather than as a servant. Considering the illiteracy of the vast majority of women at that time, it is obvious that she had been much better educated than most girls, an advantage which she was later to stress in her own writings. 'When I was fourteen years old', she writes, 'I began to consider how I might improve my time to the best advantage, not knowing at that age any thing but what reason and fancy dictated me.' Reason and fancy, helped by the learning inculcated by her parents, seem to have been fairly good instructors, for by the age of fifteen she was 'intrusted to keep a little School, and was the sole Mistress thereof'. The average girl, orphaned at so early an age, with no dowry and therefore few prospects of marriage, would probably have had to be content with the lower echelons of domestic service. Hannah, however, after two years' teaching, 'understood indifferently the smooth *Italian*, and could sing, dance and play on several sorts of Musical Instruments'. These accomplishments, not unnaturally, caught the eye of a local noblewoman:

> My extraordinary parts appear'd more splendid in the eyes of a Noble Lady in this kingdom, than really they deserv'd, who praising my works with the appellation of curious pieces of Art, was infinitely pleas'd therewith.

Hannah was engaged (or 'greedily entertained', as she puts it) as a governess to this lady's daughter. She obviously learned as much from the lady as she taught the daughter:

> Unto this honourable Person I am indebted for the *basis* or

groundwork of my Preserving and Cookery, by my observation of what she order'd to be done.

Via this lady, whose name I've been unable to discover, she also 'came acquainted with the Court, with a deportment suitable thereunto', though she does not relate further details.

This noble lady died after only a year, and Hannah moved on to another, 'no way inferior to the former', as she hastens to reassure us. It is impossible to be certain, but it is quite likely that this second lady was the Anne Wroth to whom, in 1664, she dedicated her second book, *The Cook's Guide*. Anne was the wife of Sir Henry Wroth, who came from an old Essex family and had connections with Newport, near Saffron Walden. Where they lived when Mrs Woolley started her new job is unknown, but in 1642, Henry's uncle John died and left him an estate in Chigwell, a village in west Essex about 25 miles from Newport. The Civil War was dividing the country at this time, and Henry, who was described as a 'gentleman pensioner' of Charles I, was rewarded for his loyalty to the King with a knighthood, which was conferred on him at Hereford (or possibly Chirk Castle) on September 15th, 1645. Hannah stayed with her new mistress for seven years, during which time her accomplishments increased yet more.

If, as seems almost certain, her employers were the Wroths, she had chosen people with cultivated connections. Sir Henry's aunt, Mary Wroth, was the niece of Sir Philip Sidney, and an author in her own right. Hannah obviously benefitted from the intellectual atmosphere, and acquired new skills. Although she was originally engaged as governess, 'time, and my Ladies good opinion of me' led to her becoming her mistress's 'Woman, her Stewardess, and her Scribe or Secretary'. She was, in her own words,

> a person of no mean authority in the Family. *I* kept an exact account of what was spent in the house . . . In short time I became skilful, and stayed enough to order a house, and all Offices belonging to it.

She also mentions having prepared a banquet for Charles I with her own hands, though unfortunately she does not give any further details of what must have been an impressive occasion. This anecdote further emphasizes the Royalist sympathies of her employers.

Her accomplishments were not confined to household management; she learned 'courtly phrases and graces, so how to express my self with the attendancy of a becoming air', and how to manage her tongue 'gracefully and discreetly'. She acquired all this knowledge by listening to 'that ingenious and agreeable discourse interfac'd between my Lady and Persons of Honour', by writing her mistress's letters, with the aid of all the fashionable letter-writers of the day, and by reading aloud plays and poems to her employer. As many of these were in French, 'this put me upon the understanding of that Language . . . which is as great an Ornament for young Ladies as those learned Tongues, of which the Academical *studioso* boasts a more than common understanding'. The remarks about the boastful *studioso* are typical of Hannah's attitude towards the pretensions of the male sex. She will return to the subject of languages for girls, and the manners of educated men, in her writings on education, of which more later.

As well as these intellectual activities, Hannah improved her practical abilities:

> As I gather'd how to manage my tongue gracefully and discreetly; so I thought it not irrequisite to let my hands lye idle. [She becomes slightly confused there with the double negative.] I exercised them daily in carving at Table. And when any sad accident required their help in Physick and Chyrurgery [surgery], I was ready to be assisting . . .

She gives a striking example of how her talents were exercised. At the age of twenty-two, she writes:

> I was sent by this Noble Lady to a Woman in hard labour of Child . . . by God's help those Remedies which I gave her caused her Fits to cease, and a safe Delivery followed.

With all these accomplishments, Hannah must have been an attractive prospect for wife-seekers. She did not marry until she was 24, in 1647 or possibly 1648. Conscious as always of her own gifts, she kept the suitors (whom she implies were numerous) at bay, until, as she says:

> I gained so great an esteem among the Nobility and Gentry of two Counties, that I was necessitated to yield to the importunity of one I dearly lov'd, that I might free my self from the tedious caresses of a many more.

Her husband was Benjamin Woolley, Master of the Grammar School at Newport, near Saffron Walden in Essex (where members of the Wroth family, incidentally, were living in Elizabeth I's reign). Not that much is known about Mr Woolley himself, but there is a clue as to his family background in the records of another Woolley, Robert. He went up to Christ Church, Oxford, in 1674, and described himself on the register as the son of Jeremiah Woolley of Newport, Essex, a plebeian. If, as seems almost certain, this Jeremiah was a relation – perhaps a cousin or even a younger brother – it is likely that Benjamin was of a similarly low social standing. Furthermore, it shows that the family, like Mrs Woolley herself, was adept at 'getting on'; for a plebeian to send his son to Oxford must have been quite something. One of Mrs Woolley's sons was also to go to University, probably Cambridge, and of course Benjamin had made good by becoming a schoolmaster. He had been a scholar at the Grammar School himself, before returning as Usher, or assistant master, in 1635.

The 'ffree grammer Schole' at Newport was founded in the year of the Armada, 1588, by a wealthy local lady, Mrs Joyce Frankland, as a memorial to her only son, killed in a riding accident at the age of 23. Its regulations, which we must presume Benjamin followed, give us a good idea of what boys (not girls, who had no schools) learned at this period. They enjoin that 'the master instil good manners as well as learning', and that he should be neither too severe nor 'too easily inclined to lenity'. It really was a free school, in as much as it gave children from poor homes, such as Benjamin, a real chance of acquiring a decent education. Poor boys were 'to be first admitted to the number of fifty', and the master had to show 'equal respect to rich and poor and pay the same attention to teaching both'. The school day started at six and ended at five, and the subjects were Grammar, Latin, Greek and Hebrew, with time set aside for 'recreation and innocent diversions as running, throwing darts and the bow'.

For teaching all this, Benjamin would only have received, under the terms of the benefaction, £6 13s 4d (£6.66) a year as Usher, and, when he became Master in 1644, £13 6s 8d (£13.33). If he had no assistant, he would have received the full £20 a year. Presumably the salary had risen by Benjamin's time, otherwise Hannah really would have been putting love before money – in 1686, the Master of Oundle School received £30 a year, at a time when a cookmaid might expect around £3 a year. Of course, the Woolleys would receive lodging as well, but I imagine Mrs Woolley's talents as a house-keeper came in very useful. When you add her skills as a physician, governess and secretary, she was certainly well qualified to be a good matron and general manager. In her own words, she had a great knowledge of 'the humours, inclinations, and dispositions of children', which must have come in handy in dealing with sixty or more schoolboys, not to mention her four sons, who were presumably fairly easy to handle, being as Mrs Woolley says, 'as good Children as ever Woman did bear'.

The school seems to have been a success. Mr Woolley got at least three boys scholarships to St John's, Cambridge, and Mrs Woolley says that her medical skill 'was often exercised' among their boarders. They

> fell into distempers; as Agues, Feavors, Meazles, Small-pox, Consumption and many other Diseases ... [but] unless they were desperately ill their Parents trusted me without the help of any Physician or Chirurgien ...

This passage is a good example of what Asa Wallas calls 'the frank sense of her own value that is one of her charms'. She did not just help the schoolboys, though:

> I had frequent occasion to make use of all or most of my aforenamed qualities; and what I exercis'd not within my own roof, I used among my neighbours, friends and acquaintants.

They stayed in Newport (or Newport-Pond as Mrs Woolley, along with some of her contemporaries, calls it) for another seven years, then, in 1655, they set up their own school in Hackney, then a rural village near London, rather than a suburb of it. It was already a centre of genteel education, and continued to develop as a favourite place for running private schools. It was also celebrated for its excellent turnips – several of Mrs Woolley's recipes specify '*Hackney* turneps'. 'We had above threescore Boarders,' writes Mrs Woolley, 'and there I had many more trials for my skill both home and abroad'. Illness and disease of many sorts were prevalent, especially in cities, in this period, and there was effectively no organised medical profession. Those practitioners who were available frequently had no qualifications, but they still charged enormous fees. A cure for smallpox could cost anything between £2 7s (£2.35) and £45, and a doctor could charge 2/6 (12½p) a head to bleed the servants. Thus Mrs Woolley's medical abilities must have made her very popular among neighbours, as well as with the parents of her boys, and of course she harps on her successes to remind the reader of how eminently qualified she is to give medicinal advice.

Her medicinal skill could not, however, save her husband, who died in 1661. His death seemed to have occurred among many other troubles, perhaps to have been the culminating disaster. She sums up her various setbacks in *The Gentlewoman's Companion* thus:

> As I have taken great pains for an honest livelihood, so the hand of the Almighty hath exercised me in all manner of Afflictions, by death of Parents when very young, by loss of Husband, Children, Friends, Estate, very much sickness, by which I was disenabled from my Employment.

The sickness included a severe attack of the 'palsie', or paralysis, which afflicted her some time before 1674. Whenever it occurred, it was entirely typical of Mrs Woolley to turn it to good use, as a further advertisement for her abilities:

> And for the Palsie, whether Dead or shaking, I am sure none can give better Remedies, nor know it better than I do, having bought my Experience at a dear rate; there is none who have been more afflicted with it myself, and . . . there is no Person more freer from it than my self . . . and that is very much, I being now in my Two and fiftieth year.

It is equally characteristic of her resilience that, in the year when her husband died, Hannah started her career as a writer. Presumably the death of Benjamin led to the closure of the school, and Hannah had to find some way of earning money. For her first book, *The Ladies Directory*, she acted as her own 'publisher', which in those days meant simply that it would have been sold at her own house, rather than at a bookseller's. It cost the princely sum of six shillings, and the high price brought forth another of her typically forthright and self-confident statements: 'I beseech you grudge it not, since there is in it, many Pounds worth of Skill imparted to you.' Indeed there is; the full sub-title reads:

> *Choice Experiments & Curiosities of Preserving & Candying both Fruits and Flowers. Also, An Excellent way of making Cakes, and other Comfits.*

She increases the readers' respect by telling them that she has performed 'triumphs and trophies', that is, elaborate set-pieces in pastry, 'for the Entertainment of his late Majesty, as well as for the Nobility'. Enough people were prepared to spend six shillings to warrant a second edition the following year, and Mrs Woolley was launched on her career as a professional writer.

The Ladies Directory largely consists of recipes for preserving fruits and vegetables, as its sub-title indicates. These were a common feature of the cookery books of this period, as everyone wanted to know the most successful ways to make the best of what fruits and vegetables were available. The seasons for many of them were short, and there were no freezers in which to keep them, so pickled, candied and dried produce was very common. Mrs Woolley gives recipes for preserving quinces and candying eringo, the root of sea holly, which was supposed to be an aphrodisiac – 'let it hail kissing-comfits, and snow eringoes', says Falstaff in *The Merry Wives of Windsor* – a quality which might explain why it was so popular a candidate for candying. An efficient cook could store up large amounts of preserved fruit and vegetables to see her household through the long months when there was no fresh produce to be had.

Although many cookery books had already been published, and many more were to appear in this period, Hannah stands out as one of the more prolific authors on the subject, especially when one considers that writing was still very much a male preserve. 'Gaining a Name in Print' was 'a thing as rare for a Woman to endeavour, as obtain', says Mrs Woolley, but she seems to have managed pretty well. In her first volume, she says that if it was 'so well accepted on, as it was by those who knew both her and her practice therein', she would produce a book of cookery to compliment it, 'which may be very useful to all that do delight in neat and noble Entertainments'. Presumably she was sufficiently encouraged by the book's success in reaching a second edition, and in 1664 Mrs Woolley published her second book, *The Cooks Guide*. In a later work she was to note, not without complacency, that both books 'have found very good Acceptance', so it can be assumed that her reputation as an expert on domestic matters was growing.

However, it seems clear from the book's dedication that, despite her literary success, life had not been treating Hannah very well. The dedication is to 'the Honourable and truly Vertuous Lady, Anne Wroth, Wife to the Right Worshipful Sir Henry Wroth', and is worth quoting at length:

Madam,

The Duty I owe to your Ladyship, and the rest of your Noble Family, commands more than this book is able to Express; but since ill fate hath made me altogether incapable of any Worthy return of your Love and bounty, be pleased to accept this as a Signal of what I am obliged to. I would not willingly dye while I live, nor be forgotten when I am dead; therefore have I sent forth this book, to testifie to the scandalous World, that I do not altogether spend my time idely; somewhat of benefit it may be to the young Ladies and Gentlewomen; and such I wish it . . .

Madam,

Your Honours most Faithful, Real, and most Humble Servant, Hannah Wolley [sic].

The ironic understatement with which Mrs Woolley mentions not spending her time idly is absolutely typical, as is the fulsome protestation of fidelity at the end. The reference to 'ill fate' perhaps refers to the loss of her first husband, or to illness, or both. One gains the impression that she was unable to do manual work at this period, but she was obviously still able to write.

There is also a charming dedication to Lady Wroth's daughter Mary, which I reprint not only to give the reader an impression of the obvious respect and affection which Mrs Woolley had for the family, but also of one of her aims in writing her books:

> *To the Vertuous and truly Ingenuous young Gentlewoman Mistris* Mary Wroth, *Daughter to the Right Worshipful Sir* HENRY WROTH.

> Dear Mistress,

> The sublimity of your Lady Mothers affairs I fear will not permit her very often to view this book; besides, her Ladyship needs it not, her acceptation and approbation hereof is my honour only, not her benefit; your practice will be my content, and I doubt not your own. It is a miserable thing for any Woman, though never so great, not to be able to teach her Servants; there is no fear of it in you, since you begin so soon to delight in those Sciences as may and will accomplish you; this Book I hope will afford you something; and whatever else you know in me to serve you, be pleased freely to command; I shall always be ready to express my self

> *Dear Mistress,*

> *Your unfeigned Real Servant in all Humility and affection*
> *Hannah Wolley [sic].*

This passage shows that Mrs Woolley regarded her audience as being at least partly composed of employers, as well as employees. Few of the lesser servants would be able to read, and it would be up to the mistress of the house to buy the books and pass on their message. *The Cooks Guide* contains a large number of recipes which Mrs Woolley assures the reader are all original:

> They are very Choice Receipts, and such as I have not taken up on the Credit of others, but do Commend them to you from my own Practice . . . I could have enlarged the Volume very much, had I not picked out only such as I thought to be the very best; and such as hath cost me much time, and great pains to gather together.

Mrs Woolley was perhaps displaying a little *faux-naiveté* in saying that *all* her material was original. Copying of recipes from one book to another was quite common, and Robert May, one of the most celebrated chefs and writers of the period, mentions, in the dedication to his *The Accomplish't Cook,*

> those already extant Authors [who] have trac't but one common beaten road, repeating for the main what others have in the same homely manner done before them.

It must be admitted that almost all cookery writers said the same about their rivals, but most of them borrowed from each other. Later in her career, Mrs Woolley herself admits to 'borrowing', but comparison with other books of the period shows that she was no worse an offender than others. *The Cooks Guide* has proved a major source of recipes for this selection – I found Lemon Cream and Whipped Syllabub in it, for instance, which are two of the best desserts in the book.

Mrs Woolley published no further books for six years. It may well be that she went back into service, but there is one important piece of evidence to suggest that she might not have needed money so urgently at this period: she remarried. On 16th April 1666, five months before the Great Fire, Hannah married Francis Challinor, a widower aged about forty-five, of the parish of St Margaret's, Westminster. We do not know anything about him apart from where he lived, and the fact that he was described as 'Gent.' on the marriage license. Perhaps his occupation did not provide as many occasions as Benjamin's for the exercise, and subsequent advertisement, of Hannah's manifold talents. Mrs Woolley did not use her new husband's surname in any of her books, continuing to sign herself Hannah Woolley or Wolley, or Woolly, or Wolly, occasionally adding 'alias Chaloner'. In all this she showed the easy-going attitude to spelling which was such a feature of the age. Presumably she kept her first married name for sound commercial reasons – there was no point in throwing away a successful and recognised name. It was certainly not a disparagement of her second husband: 'though I have passed through many more Afflictions and Troubles then thousands of my Sex', she wrote in 1674, 'yet I never had an ill Husband . . . (on the contrary) I have been married to two Worthy, Eminent and brave persons'.

That use of 'have been' might indicate that by 1674, Francis Challinor was dead, which would explain why Mrs Woolley started to publish again in the 1670s. In 1670, she published her third book, a collection of recipes whose full title must be allowed to speak for itself:

The Queen-like Closet,
OR
RICH CABINET:
Stored with all manner of
RARE RECEIPTS
FOR
Preserving, Candying, and Cookery.
Very Pleasant and Beneficial to all
Ingenious Persons of the *Female Sex.*

The unusual name was probably a calculated attempt to exploit the success of the popular *Queen's Closet* of a few years earlier, from which Mrs Woolley was later to borrow ideas herself. The dedication of *The Queen-like Closet* is interesting in that it shows both Mrs Woolley's increased social standing, and gives a glimpse of how society itself was reshaping in the second half of the seventeenth century. The book is dedicated

> TO THE TRULY VIRTUOUS AND My much Honoured Friend Mrs *GRACE BUZBY*, Daughter to the late SIR *HENRY CARY*, Knight Banneret; and WIFE to Mr. *ROBERT BUZBY*, Gentleman, and Woollen Draper of *LONDON*.

She calls Mrs Buzby her 'friend', so she is obviously not just an employer. It is noteworthy that the daughter of a knight banneret – that is, someone knighted for bravery on the field of battle in the presence of the King – would marry a woollen draper. This cross-breeding of the aristocratic and merchant families must have helped to restore fortunes to the former, while giving the latter a touch of class. Sir Henry, incidentally, like Sir Henry Wroth, was knighted by Charles I during the Civil War, which shows once again Mrs Woolley's attraction to old Royalist families and their connections.

The prefatory remarks to *The Queen-like Closet* seem to suggest that her writing was proving popular, and Mrs Woolley as usual stresses the high quality of her new work:

> I presume those Books which have passed from me formerly, have got me some little credit and esteem among you. But there being so much time past since they were Printed, that methinks, I hear some of you say, I wish Mrs *Wolley* [sic] would put forth some New Experiments; and to say the Truth, I have been importun'd by divers of my Friends and Acquaintance to do so . . . I [being] very desirous to serve you, do now present you with this Queen-like Closet: I do assure you it is worthy of the title it bears, for the very precious things you will find in it.

The reading public seems to have thought it worth buying, for it ran into five editions.

Not content with the second edition of *The Queen-like Closet*, which appeared in 1672, in the same year Mrs Woolley published *The Ladies Delight*, which was in effect a revised reprint, in one volume, of her first two books from the 1660s. She uses the same frontispiece, an engraving of women performing various domestic tasks, but a different title-page description, presumably so that the reader might (at first glance) mistake it for an entirely new work. Her publisher complicates matters by giving his readers *three* books in one: not only *The Ladies Delight*, or a *Rich Closet of Choice Experiments & Curiosities, Containing the Art of Preserving & Candying*, but *The Exact Cook; or, The Art of Dressing all sorts of Flesh, Fowl and Fish* and *The Ladies Physical Closet: Or, Excellent Receipts and Rare Waters for Beautifying the Face and Body*. (This last may have been a publisher's filler, and was very probably not written by Mrs Woolley.) Mrs Woolley added some more recipes, and all in all, it must have made a splendid Christmas present.

The prefatory letter to *The Ladies Delight* shows Hannah in agreement with Sherlock Holmes, who did not count modesty as one of the virtues. This book, she says, 'containeth more than all the Books that ever I saw Printed in this Nature, they being rather Confounders, than Instructors'. Furthermore, 'they are very Choice Receipts . . . from my own Practice, who have had the Honour to perform such things for the Entertainment of His late MAJESTY, as well as for the Nobility'. Perhaps not *all* from her own practice: Mrs Woolley, like almost every other writer of the period, including Isaak Walton, for instance, was not averse to borrowing more or less extensively from other practitioners. As we shall see, she makes a virtue of it in her next book. We do not know if she ever worked for Charles I, though as she tells us she prepared a banquet for him 'with her own hands', she may well have been in charge of the kitchen when he visited her employers. Plenty of cooks (and others) claimed his patronage. She knew at least one member of the nobility, Lady Wroth, well enough to dedicate the book to her.

The title page of *The Exact Cook* makes it yet more clear at which market Mrs Woolley was aiming: 'Excellent Receipts for Cookery . . . Whereby Noble Persons, and others in their *Hospitalities*, may be gratified in their *Gusto's*'. It is clear that Mrs Woolley's recipes could only be enjoyed by people with comfortable incomes, but she doesn't boast of the lavish expense of her dishes in the way that Robert May does in his *Accomplish't Cook*. The 'Delicates' in his book were 'of such high prices, which only these *Noblesses Hospitalities* did reach to'. Indeed, she makes fun of the cost and trouble taken by 'some rare whimsical *French* Cook' to produce a dish (one of May's, in fact) which she dismisses as 'a Miscellaneous hodg-podg of studied vanity'. Still, Mrs Woolley did not scruple to adapt some of May's less extravagant recipes for her own books.

As well as the recipes in *The Exact Cook*, the book is interesting for the medicinal 'receipts' in *The Ladies Delight*, which show Mrs Woolley's fascination with 'physic', as she called it. As she knew from her own experience, it was a good thing to be well versed in the medical arts, given the quality of 'professional' medical care at the time. However, it is difficult to believe that many of her prescriptions were successful, unless by accident. If no more efficacious than those of other contemporary writers, they were perhaps slightly less horrible, on the whole. For example, an anonymous recipe of 1654 for 'a very good Pomatum', starts: 'Take the fat of a young Dog, one pound . . .' She is not quite as bad as that, but a remedy for 'the Red Flux' is pretty brutal: 'Take Sperma Coeti [a waxy by-product of the sperm whale] and drink it, and truss yourself up with a piece of Black Cotton.' However, Mrs Woolley does at least have some consideration for her patients' feelings; after prescribing a mixture of apples, paper and coal grit to cure 'the Bloody Flux', she adds 'Eat of it, as your stomach will give you leave'.

Many of the remedies are very homely – for instance, a 'Stinking Breath, which comes from the Stomach', can be cured with repeated doses of white wine boiled with cummin seeds, and hair can be made to smell pleasant with 'a Rare Sweet-Powder for the Hair, made from starch, rosemary, rosewater, and powder of Damask-Roses'. A more serious note is sounded by a recipe, which would have been very topical then, 'to take away the signes of the small Pox':

> Take some Perma-cittee [sperma coeti], and put to it twice as much of the best Bees-wax, melt them together, then spread it upon Leather like a Mask, and cut holes for your Eyes and Mouth, then lay it on your face, and keep it on Night and Day.

The most extravagant recipes, for which the most extravagant claims were made, were undoubtedly distilled waters. Any housewife with pretensions to being accomplished would have her own 'limbeck', or still, and indeed, the frontispiece to *The Ladies Delight* shows ladies using one. Among the 'waters' listed in *The Ladies Delight* is one called simply 'a very rare water', which was 'guaranteed' to have cured many consumptions 'which the Doctors hath given over'. Making it involves plucking a live chicken (no easy feat), and finding among other things ambergris (another product of the sperm whale, used in making perfumes), musk, 'twelve pennyworth of leaf-gold' and (most difficult to locate of all) 'seven graines of Unicorns Horn'. This last ingredient explains why it was such a rare water, and perhaps also supplied Mrs Woolley with an insurance against dissatisfied customers; if they complained that the water did not work, she could blame them for not adding the unicorn's horn. A water with a much wider range of application, as well as being easier to manufacture, was walnut water. This, Mrs Woolley says, heals dropsies and palsies, helps the eyes, 'helpeth the

Conception in a Woman', 'driveth out all Corruption and inward bruises' and 'killeth Worms in the Body.' Last but not least, it can also rescue wine which has gone off. Recipes for it were still being printed at the end of the eighteenth century.

Undoubtedly the most fantastic of all the preparations in *The Ladies Delight* is snail water. The recipe deserves to be given in full:

> Take a peck of Snails (with the houses on their backs), have in readyness a good fire of Charcoal well kindled, make a hole in the midst of the first, and cast in your Snails, and still renew your fire till the Snails be well roasted, then rub them with a fair Cloth, till you have rubbed off all the green that will come off, then put them in a morter and bruise them, (shells and all) then take Clarie, Cellandine, Burrage, Scabeous, Bugloss, five-leaved Grass; and if you feel your self hot, Wood-Sorrel; of every one of these a good handful, with five tops of Angelico; these herbs being all bruised in a Morter, put them in a sweet earthen Pot, with five quarts of White-Wine, and two quarts of Ale, let them steep all night, then put them in a Limbeck; let the herbs be in the bottom of the pot, and the Snails upon the herbs, and upon the Snails, put a pint of Earth-Worms slit, and clean washed; then put upon them four ounces of Anni-seeds or Fennel-seeds, which you please, well bruised, and five great handfuls of Rose-mary flowers well picked, two or three Races of Turmerick thin sliced, Hartshorn and Ivory, of each four ounces well steeped in a quart of White-Wine, till it be like a Jelly; then put them in order into the Limbeck, and draw it forth with care.

No doubted exhausted by writing out the recipe, Mrs Woolley forgot to mention what it is to be used for, but luckily in a later edition of *The Queen-like Closet* she explained that snail water is good for consumptions.

Her next work, *The Gentlewoman's Companion*, published in 1673, was perhaps her greatest, and, to judge by the title-page, certainly her most ambitious. She tells us that it took nearly seven years to write, which is hardly surprising when one considers that (in her own words) it is

> a *Universal Companion* and *Guide* to the Female Sex, in all *Relations*, *Companies*, and *states* of *Life* even from Child-hood down to *old-age*; and from the Lady at the *Court* to the Cook-maid in the *Country*.

Even the ever-confident Mrs Woolley seemed to be daunted by the task:

> I know I may be censured by many for undertaking this great Design, in presenting to all of our Sex a compleat Directory, and that which contains several Sciences: deeming it a Work for a *Solomon* . . .

but the mood obviously didn't last long:

> I doubt not but that judicious persons will esteem this essay of mine, when they have read the Book, and weighed it well; and if so, I shall the less trouble myself what the ignorant do or say.

Its publishing history shows some of the problems affecting authors in the days before copyright law existed. A publisher called Dorman Newman asked her to write a cookery book and general domestic treatise. She agreed, and after much labour sent him the manuscript. However, for some reason he delayed in publishing it, and further annoyed Mrs Woolley by giving the proofs to someone else to correct. She protested, they made a new agreement, and she corrected the new version and wrote the introduction. Then he complicated matters further by refusing to pay her any of the money due under the new agreement. She may have tried to take him to court, but it seems unlikely that she would have met with success, as at this period books were deemed the sole property of the publisher. To make up for this, Mrs Woolley attacked him in a 'Supplement' dated 1674, which was appended to further editions of her *Queen-like Closet*. History doesn't relate whether she ever got any money for *The Gentlewoman's Companion*, but the second edition of 1675 was brought out by a different publisher, so Newman couldn't have made that much profit from its success. (Incidentally, he was declared bankrupt in 1694.) Mrs Woolley seems to have had trouble finding and keeping a reliable publisher – Peter Dring produced her first two books, Richard Lowndes ('a sincere honest dealer') her third, N Crouch her fourth and Newman *and* one Edward Thomas her fifth. Obviously, it was something of a free-for-all in the cut-throat bookselling world of the Restoration, a situation which many would maintain has not changed since.

In her introduction to *The Gentlewoman's Companion*, Mrs Woolley mentions once again that her other books have found 'very good Acceptance', and, 'at the desire of the Bookseller and earnest intreaties of very many worthy Friends', she has produced another one. This work covers a wide range of subjects, including education, deportment, table manners, letter-writing, and instructions for all manner of servants from governesses to scullery-maids, as well as a collection of recipes and remedies for various illnesses. She obtained her information on all these matters partly by long experience, and partly from the study of other books. The introduction gives us a good idea of her working methods. In matters of cuisine, she writes,

> I will not deny that I have made some use of that Excellent Book, *The Queens Closet*, *May's Cookery* . . . and what other Books I thought

pertinent and proper to make up a Compleat Book, that might have a Universal Usefulness.

In the same way, when researching her chapters on behaviour, she has had

> the concurrent advice and direction of the most able Professors and Teachers, both here and beyond the Seas; yet durst not be so airy and light in my Treatise about Ladies Love and Courtship as some of the *French* Authors have been, but have taken out of them what I found most taking with our *English* Gentry.

(This adaptation of French manners to English tastes is parallelled in the culinary practice of the time, when French food was becoming popular in Britain.) Despite all the authorities she quotes, there is much in the book, she says, 'that I have not met with in any Language, but are the Product of my Thirty years Obervations and Experience'. The sheer scope of the book makes it worth reading, and quoting from in more detail.

Mrs Woolley was passionately interested in telling women every thing they needed to know about almost everything, for starkly practical reasons. She recognised that, without a good range of abilities, women could not hope to succeed in marriage, the main means by which women could hope to improve their situation. Thus she emphasizes the need for women, of all classes, to have a good practical knowledge of housekeeping – how to cook, prepare and administer remedies, order servants correctly – as well as decent intellectual accomplishments. Thus equipped, women could expect to make good marriages, rather than remain the 'companion to grooms and footboys'. The range of abilities housewives were expected to have was very great, especially if they were to keep up a country establishment. Gervase Markham, in his popular (and much imitated and borrowed from) *Countrey Contentments* (1615) lists some of the essential country skills: 'Phisycke, Surgerie, Extraction of Oyles, Banquetting-stuffe . . . Conceited Secrets, Distillations . . . Brewing, Baking' and more. He also gives an interesting reason for women learning to cook: if a wife cannot cook, she 'may not by the laws of strict Justice challenge the freedom of Marriage, because indeed she can then but perform halfe her vow; for she may love and obey, but shee cannot serve and keep him'.

Mrs Woolley, it is clear, was well able to serve and keep not only her husband, but everyone for whom she was responsible, and in *The Gentlewoman's Companion* passed on a great deal of inform-ation to enable others to do the same. 'I look upon the end of Life to be Usefulness', she writes, which could almost be her motto, and she certainly gave an enormous amount of useful advice to 'all Young Ladies, Gentlewomen, and all Maidens, whatever' in her book. She covers the fields of medicine, polite behaviour and deportment (including table-manners), the correct education of girls and young women, and the Servant Question (both how to treat them and what their duties should be). She also gives examples of polite dialogues and letters to serve as model for the aspirant conversationalist and letter-writer.

The first subject with which Mrs Woolley deals in *The Gentlewoman's Companion* is the education of women. Obviously, the whole book is about the education of women, in the broadest sense, but it is unusual in devoting space to the fostering of the intellect as well. She held strong views on this, and her ideas were very advanced for her time. Indeed, her insistence on the proper education of women is striking in a period when, in some parts of the country, eighty per cent of women were not even literate, let alone learned. For practical reasons, she wanted parents to

> endeavour the gentile [gentle] education of their Daughters, encouraging them to learn whatever opportunity offers, worthy [of] a good estimation. *For riches hath wings, and will quickly fly away*; or Death comes and removes the Parents, leaving the Children to the tuition of merciless and unconscionable Executors . . .

Perhaps Mrs Woolley, whose parents died young, is speaking here from personal experience. She must also have seen the effects of the Civil War on family life and fortunes – a great many families, both Royalist and Parliamentarian, were ruined. As a result, plenty of women had been stranded in the predicament she describes, with no means of support and no qualifications for earning their keep, and it is to them, perhaps more than anyone else, that she addresses her advice. She describes them as 'Gentlewomen, who though wellborn, are notwithstanding by indigency neccessitated to serve some person of quality', and if they are ill-equipped to serve in this way, she blames it, at least in part, on the negligence (born perhaps of snobbery) of their parents, who:

> slight those arts which may not be only ornamental, but beneficial to their Children hereafter, vainly imagining that poverty will never approach their Gates; by which cross mistake their Daughters are often exposed to great hardships, many times contenting themselves to serve as Chamber-maids, because they have not the Accomplishments of a Waiting-woman, or an House-keeper.

Hence the pressing need for education of women, which, it becomes clear, Mrs Woolley thinks is deliberately provided for boys while being denied to girls. This radical attitude provokes her into fiery language on the subject:

> I cannot but complain of, and must condemn the great negligence of Parents, in letting the fertile ground of their Daughters lie fallow, yet send the barren Noddles of their sons to the University, where they stay for no other purpose than to fill their empty Sconces with idle notions to make a noise in the Country.

She expands this idea that women have 'fertile' minds, ripe for development, while men's are sterile, and gives some sound feminist reasons as to why men prevent women from being educated:

> Vain man is apt to think we were meerly intended for the World's propagation, and to keep its humane inhabitants sweet and clean; but . . . had we the same Literature, they would find our brains as fruitful as our bodies. Hence I am induced to believe, we are debarred from the knowledge of humane learning, lest our pregnant Wits should rival the towering conceits of our insulting Lords and Masters.

Mrs Woolley wanted girls to learn French, Italian and Latin, especially the latter, as it would help them to speak correct English, and also to match those 'Fops of Rhetorick' and 'spawns of non-intelligency' who delight in using lots of pretentious Latinate words and risk 'the spraining of their tongues, and splay-footing their own mouths, if they can but cramp a Young Gentlewoman's intellect'. Girls should read Divinity (naturally), but also romances such as Sir Philip Sidney's *Arcadia*, because it contains 'Generosity, Gallantry and Virtue'. They should also, one assumes, read the works of Mrs Woolley, especially *The Gentlewoman's Companion*, which has a whole section on children's behaviour.

A combination of polite learning such as this, and the practical skills already described, would help ensure that, in the event of a family disaster, a girl could at least earn her living as a governess or secretary/companion, as Mrs Woolley herself had, a position from which respectable marriage could be obtained. Turned loose on the world with no abilities, women might have to be content with life as a maidservant, or similar, from which a further descent sometimes occurred. Daniel Defoe, who was, incidentally, a later and more celebrated resident of Hackney, described, early in the eighteenth century, the numbers of young maidservants who had come to London for work and, finding none, were forced to 'prostitute their bodies or starve'. In a society where a woman's best chances of survival were in marriage, Mrs Woolley makes it obvious that a girl should be educated, in practical and 'polite' subjects, to make herself as good a prospect as possible. Her great strength is that she can accept this as a hard fact of life, without assuming that women must demean themselves in achieving it. It is also clear, although she does not say so openly, that she believed in giving women a grounding in intellectual matters for their own sake; her attitude seems to be that, even though women were dependent on the favour of men, they should at least show that they could be their equals, were society differently organised.

Mrs Woolley also held quite advanced views on methods of education, in that she disapproved of the widespread practice of corporal punishment. 'Blows', she states in *The Gentlewoman's Companion* 'are fitter for beasts than rational creatures'. However, she did not advocate an over-lenient approach, telling governesses that they should be 'the incessant tormentors of Sloth' in their pupils.

Having dealt with education, Mrs Woolley turns to dress. Naturally, a young woman should be well turned out, but she should not blindly follow all the fads of fashion. Indeed, Mrs Woolley is rather acid about fashion, and writes bluntly of its more absurd manifestations: 'I know not, but that the fashion of wearing Farthingales of old, were not politicky invented to hide the shame of great Bellis [bellies] unlawfully puft up.' (A farthingale was a kind of hoop, especially popular in the Elizabethan period, which was worn under the skirt to spread it out.)

Behaviour in polite society occupies Mrs Woolley's attention a good deal in *The Gentlewoman's Companion*, and although she gives some instructions on 'the gait or Gesture' and 'the Government of the Eye', she concentrates especially on deportment at the dinner party. Dinner in the late seventeenth century was much nearer midday than the evening, though the hour was gradually advancing – Cromwell (whose favourite dish, by the way, was said to have been roast veal with oranges) dined at around eleven o'clock in the morning – but less than a century later we find the poet Alexander Pope refusing an invitation because he feels too old to adjust to the fashionably late dinner time of four o'clock. Then, as now, dinners could be a chance for elegant and lavish display, not just of food, but of furnishings. A book published in 1682 gives details of how an elegant dining-room should look:

> The Rome well wanscotted about . . . [and] hung with pictures of all sorts, as History, Landskips, Fancyes, &c. Long Table in the middle, either square to draw out in Leaves, or Long, or Round or oval . . . Side tables, or court cubberts for cups and glasses to drink in, Spoons, Sugar Box, Viall and Cruces for Viniger, Oyle and Mustard pot.

There should also be brass or pewter cisterns for cooling beer and wine, and elaborate upholstery: 'A Turky table cover, or carpett of cloth or Leather printed', for instance, the chairs in 'Turkey work, Russia or calves Leather'. There should be a few flower pots in the windows, and a 'Long seeing Glass' as well, and the dining room should open onto a 'Faire with-drawing Rome', well furnished, of course.

To match the elegance of the surroundings, the entertainments given in high society could be very lavish. The historian Thomas Fuller tells a story about a famous dwarf from Rutland, one Jeffrey, called 'the least man of the least county of England'. He was only one and a half feet tall, and was 'presented in a cold baked pie to king Charles and queen Mary at an entertainment'. Another similar display, this time involving live birds and animals, is described on p. 67.

Despite the care lavished on the dining room and the entertainments, behaviour in it might not be very genteel. The voluminous instructions which Mrs Woolley gives concerning table manners are so detailed in their proscriptions that one wonders just how degenerate they were in the Restoration. This was, after all, at a time when the aristocracy were noted for their loose morals and lax manners. Pepys tells a story about Sir Charles Sedley, a famous dramatist, wit and boon companion of King Charles, being fined £500 for disporting himself with some friends, very drunk, on the balcony of the Cock tavern, making lewd and blasphemous gestures and speeches to a shocked, but appreciative crowd below. This was perhaps an extreme case, but even so, it still comes as a slight shock to read Mrs Woolley's remark that 'In carving at your own Table . . . it will appear very comely and decent to use a Fork'. It should be remembered that in the seventeenth century, all the dishes forming one course, and there could easily be twenty of them, were put on the table at once, and the diners helped themselves to what they wanted, or, if they were polite, helped their neighbours. Thus the diner was dependent on his or her own ruthlessness, or the gentility of other guests, to obtain particular delicacies, or even to get enough to eat. Mrs Woolley cautions ladies against reaching across people to get at the food, and in general her suggestions for a lady's behaviour 'if you are invited abroad' are worth quoting in some detail, as an illustration of contemporary habits.

'The first thing you are to observe, is to keep your Body strait in the Chair, and do not lean your Elbows on the Table.' You should not display 'any ravenous gesture', or 'fix your eyes too greedily on the meat before you'. Neither should you 'mump it, mince it, nor bridle the head, as if you either disliked the meat or the company'. As for eating itself, you should not try to appear genteel by picking at your food. Mrs Woolley illustrates the perils of this sort of behaviour in a brief anecdote of social humiliation:

> An old-fashion Gentlewoman I have heard of, who because she would seem (being invited to a Feast) to be a slender eater, fed heartily at home (before she went) on a piece of powder'd [salted] beef and cabbage; by chance a fleak thereof fell on her Ruff, and not perceiving it, went so where she was invited; being observed to eat little or nothing, a Gentlewoman askt her why she did not eat; Indeed, Madam, said she, I did eat (before I came forth) a whole pestle [leg] of a Lark to my Breakfast, and that I think hath deprived me of my appetite. The witty Gentlewoman presently replied, I am easily induced to believe you fed on that Bird; for on your Ruff I see you have brought a feather of him with you.

Thus, adds Mrs Woolley sternly, you 'may make yourself the subject of publick laughter'. Of course, it is possible to err too much in the opposite direction:

> Do not baul out aloud for anything you want; as, I would have some of that; I like not this; I hate Onions; Give me no Pepper . . .

Instead, one should whisper softly to a servant, that 'he or she may without noise supply your wants'. Not making a noise is also important when it comes to the mechanics of eating:

> Close your lips when you eat; talk not when you have meat in your mouth; and do not smack like a Pig, nor make any other noise which shall prove ungrateful to the company . . . Fill not your mouth so full, that your cheeks shall swell like a pair of *Scotch*-bag-pipes . . .

The same sort of rules apply to drinking, too:

> It is very uncomely to drink so large a draught, that your breath is almost gone . . . nor let it go down too hastily, lest it force you to an extream cough, or bring it up again, which would be a great rudeness to nauseate the whole Table; and this throwing down your liquor as into a Funnel, would be an action fitter for a Jugler than a Gentlewoman.

Further useful pieces of information include rulings on how to serve various different foods – if you are serving fish in pastry, 'it is proper enough to touch it with your knife; if otherwise, with your fork and spoon'; while if you are helping yourself to olives, 'use your spoon, and not your fork, lest you become the laughter of the whole Table'. It is 'uncivil to rub your teeth in company, or to pick them at or after meals'; and it is even more uncivil to criticise or find fault with any dish of meat or sawce during the repast, or more especially at another's Table; or to ask what such a Joint or such a Fowl cost; or to trouble your self and others with perpetual discourses of Bills of Fare, that being a sign of a foolish Epicure.

Apart from giving the impression that it was common to criticize the food at one's *own* table, this passage shows that the traditional English habit of regarding any discussion of the food as the height of bad manners was already asserting itself.

While the instructions for eating the food correctly may sound daunting, it must have been worse to be one of those who prepared and served it. *The Gentlewoman's Companion* is full of advice for servants and those who employ them, and Mrs Woolley pays particular attention to those working in the kitchen, or generally associated with producing food. She voices some complaints about servants in general which would have sounded familiar immediately after the First and Second World Wars, and perhaps even now, among those who can still afford to keep them: 'If you find you have a bad or unfaithful Servant (as nowadays there are too many, more than ever) . . .' She singles out cooks especially: 'It is a common thing now-adays for cook-maids to ask great Wages, although they are concious themselves of their inability of performing almost anything . . .'

Her advice to any woman who wants to become an 'absolute', that is, a perfect, cook-maid, in a great or good house, is comprehensive; you should know how to dress every sort of meat and sauce, and be 'curious in garnishing your Dishes, and making all manner of Pickles', as well as ensuring, in the days before winter feed for livestock, let alone deep-freezes, that 'your Meat taint not for want of good salting'. Just as important, though, is economy: you should save 'what is left of that you have dressed, of which you make both handsome and toothsome Dishes again'. On a practical note, and once again probably speaking from experience, she advises the cook not to 'lay all your Wages on your back, but lay up something against sickness, and an hundred other Casualties'.

The under cook-maid also receives instruction, mostly to learn by observation of her superiors, and to be 'ingenious and willing to learn'. But there is more specific advice as well – 'though your employment be greasie and smutty . . . let it be your care to keep yourself clean'. Morally as well as literally, it seems:

Beware of Gossips, for they will misadvise you; beware of the sollicitations of the flesh, for they will undo you; and though you may have mean thoughts of yourself, and think none will meddle with such as you; it is a mistake, *Hungry Dogs will eat dirty Puddings*; and

I myself have known a brave Gallant to fall foul with the Wench of the Skullery . . .

Despite the hard work and long hours, life in service still had a great deal to recommend it. An ordinary living-in maid in the mid-seventeenth century could expect about £2 a year, and by diligence might rise to become personal servant to her mistress, on a wage of about £4. The money was not the most important consideration, though; an indoor servant usually received food, shelter, probably a livery, and cast-off clothing, which in a wealthy family could be worth a great deal. Diet was perhaps the area in which the divide between living-in servants and other labourers is most obvious. On farms as well as big houses, servants could expect to eat meat or fish almost every day, as well as pies, puddings, fruit and vegetables, and so on. A day-labourer in the fields, paid around a shilling (5p) a day, ate a diet little changed from the Middle Ages, except that, due to inflation, he ate less of it. Black bread, porridge, cabbage, parsnips, 'messes' and perhaps a little meat or fish very occasionally, and then usually salted, not fresh. But at least the rural labourer could grow some of his own food; town-dwellers had to pay for everything, and consequently their diet was even worse.

Another matter which Mrs Woolley touches on in *The Gentlewoman's Companion* is health. She expected all responsible women to have some knowledge of physic, and in nearly all her books there are a few remedies. (The most extended treatment of the subject is in *The Ladies Delight* of 1672, from which extracts have already been given.) She had learned it and practised it herself, and had cured herself of the 'palsie', and probably of other ailments too. In the introduction to *The Gentlewoman's Companion* she says that there is no way her sex

can be more useful in their Generation than having a competent skill in Physick and Chirurgery, a competent Estate to distribute it, and a Heart willing thereunto.

It is perhaps typical of Mrs Woolley that she rates the practical advantages of a 'competent Estate' equally with a willing heart. Knowledge of preventative medicine was just as important as the ability to cure illnesses, though, and in *The Gentlewoman's Companion* she stresses the importance of diet alongside physic. She tells us which foodstuffs are 'cooling' or 'hot', and what effect different spices and herbs have. She also tells us the pros and cons of eating sugar, widely used in cooking at the time, and some of her remarks on this subject, unlike her many of her medicines, sound quite modern:

the brownest or coarsest is most cleansing, and is good for abstertions in diseases of the Breast and Lungs . . . [but] the immoderate use thereof is dangerous; for it will rot the Teeth, and taint the Breath, engender Jaundies and Consumptions; and Physicians verily believe, that the major part of those who die of the Consumption in the City (the constantly great numbers whereof may be seen in the Weekly Bills of Mortality) are such who eat Confections, and such-like sweet things immoderately. And since I have spoken of sugar, pray take special notice of this remark, That the most part of our finest Sugar, and which is most coveted, is refined and whitened by the means of the Lee of Lime; how prejudicial that may be to the body, I will leave it to the Rational to consider.

Lime is certainly a more dangerous artificial additive than the average E-number, and Mrs Woolley's warning should ensure that we don't become too nostalgic for the period.

The other chapters of *The Gentlewoman's Companion* include model letters and dialogues. An example of the latter is between a 'lying and impertinent Traveller' and his witty female companion, in which the lady naturally has the last laugh. Both the dialogues and the letters were designed to improve the speaking and writing skills of the reader, while inculcating some useful precepts: the moral of the above-mentioned dialogue is not to boast about things of which you are ignorant. She regarded letter-writing as a neglected art: 'I meet with Letters my self sometimes, that I could even tear them as I read them, they are so full of impertinence, and so tedious.' To improve this state of affairs, she supplies model letters on a wide variety of subjects, such as the propriety of using artificial beauty-patches (arguments for and against), and the delicate matter of 'How to set about a dear female-friend whom you suspect of any youthful excursions'. She also gives an example of a proposal of marriage and the polite refusal of the offer.

On the subject of marriage, Mrs Woolley sensibly tells the reader that you should not be 'induced to marry one you have either abhorrency or loathing to'. Although this may sound rather obvious, in the context of marriages usually arranged by relatives on financial and/or dynastic grounds, it is in fact quite courageous, if Utopian, advice. No doubt she reckoned that if a girl learned everything in *The Gentlewoman's Companion*, she would be able, like Mrs Woolley herself, to take her pick of husbands.

It is clear that by this time Mrs Woolley was living in the heart of London. In 1674, according to an advertisement in the 'Supplement' to *The Queen-like Closet*, she was to be found 'at Mr Richard Woolley's House in the Old Bailey in Golden Cup Court'. Mr

Woolley was probably one of her sons; he is described as a 'Master of Arts, and Reader at St Martin's, Ludgate'. To obtain the degree of Master of Arts he must have been at one of the Universities, like his relation Richard, though it is not certain which one. This relatively elevated intellectual position is a sign of an intelligent mother, who knew how to educate her children. In 1675, the second edition of *The Gentlewoman's Companion* appeared, and an advertisement, once again, shows that she had moved house, this time only a few yards west, to East Harding Street, between Shoe Lane and Fetter Lane. Here she continued to sell 'remedies for several Distempers, at reasonable Rates', including 'Doctor *Sermon's* most Famous, Safe, *Cathartique* and *Diuratique* Pills', which cured General Monk of the dropsy in 1669. (It is perhaps unfair to mention that he died in 1670). As well as medicines, Mrs Woolley sold practical advice. In the 'Supplement', dated 1674, added to *The Queen-like Closet* she writes as follows:

> If any of you shall desire to be further informed than I can possibly direct in Writing; or to confirm themselves in what they have already made Trial of, if you please to give your selves the trouble as to come to me, I shall give you the best assistance I can in any of those things I profess to teach, and for a competent gratuity . . . For if my Pen can reach you well, how much better would my Tongue and Hands do? . . . Therefore I beseech you let it be thus;
>
> *Be pleased to afford me some of your Mony;*
>
> *And*
>
> *I will repay you with my pains and Skill*
>
> That I judge to be fair on both sides.

Another service she provided was that of domestic employment agency. She was an obvious candidate for such a job: her years of service, and writings on the subject, qualified her perfectly. Not only did she train aspiring servants, however, she would recommend those in need of jobs to her many friends, providing that they were

> ingenious and deserving, or obliging in their disposition; neat and cleanly in their Habit; not too costly but decent, lively Spirited, not bold . . .

As well as all that, they had to give 'a good account of their parentage', which seems to show that Mrs Woolley was concerned to provide only highest quality of servants. At a time when competition for the best posts, always keen, had been increased by the fashion for keeping a French maid (along with drinking French wines, eating French dishes and learning French dances), it must have paid to be as well qualified as possible.

The Supplement, mentioned above, was typically subtitled *A Little of Everything*. It contained more recipes for cooking, pickling and preserving many different foods, and curing all manner of ailments – in many respects the mixture as before. It was reprinted in 1675. In the same year, Mrs Woolley published her last recorded work, *The Accomplish'd Lady's Delight*. Or, to be more accurate, she may have done, as it does not bear her name, and it is attributed to her only on the basis of its similarity to her other works. It includes the usual range of recipes for preserving, candying and cooking, and physic, but is not on the same scale as *The Gentlewoman's Companion*. The most interesting aspect of the book is that it contains a section of 'experiments in angling', with a frontispiece showing a lady in the act of landing a fish. If it could be proved that the book really was by Mrs Woolley, this interest in angling would add a little more to the reader's impression of her character.

After the flood of new works and new editions of the old ones between 1672 and 1675, Mrs Woolley seems to fade from the scene. No new books appeared under her name, though those already in print continued to do well, some being reprinted into the eighteenth century. Whether she died around this time is not known – there is no record of the date of her death, or where she is buried. Indeed, there is really no physical trace of her left at all. The last place in which we know she lived is now an office block. However, her books remain, and I hope they help fulfil her wish, expressed in 1672, that: 'I would not willingly dye while I live nor be forgotten when I am dead'. This introduction to her life and works might best be concluded by some characteristically forthright verses with which she ended *The Gentlewoman's Companion*:

> Ladies, I hope your pleas'd, and so shall I
> If what I've writ, you may be gainers by:
> If not; it is your fault, it is not mine,
> Your benefit in this I do design . . .
> The Mony you shall pay for this my Book,
> You'l not repent of, when in it you look.
> No more at present to you I shall say,
> But wish you all the happiness I may.

THE RECIPES: AN INTRODUCTION

THESE recipes, although seventeenth-century in origin, do *not* attempt exactly to recreate the meals eaten at the time. What we eat and drink is intimately connected with our living conditions: how much money we have, where we live, how well we can exploit natural resources. We cannot reproduce seventeenth-century dishes because we cannot recall the seventeenth century itself. Perhaps more importantly, we should not *want* to. The past is another of our natural resources, and should be explored creatively, not just imitated. Mrs Woolley's recipes are the product of her own time, but they are also excellent in themselves, which is why they are worth our attention. After all, the most important thing about any cookery book is the quality of the recipes. The proof of the pudding is, quite literally, in the eating.

And the eating, in the seventeenth century, was taken very seriously. Gervase Markham, for one, knew what food should be like:

> wholesome and prepared at due howers, and Cookt with care and diligence, lest it be rather to satisfie nature than our affections, and apter to kill hunger then revive new appetites . . .

As I've already mentioned, I feel that, starting during the reign of Victoria, English food more and more became simply a means of killing hunger, and the idea that it should be actively enjoyed and should 'revive new appetites' was gradually lost. Hence my interest in the older and more appetising tradition of the seventeenth century. Markham's comments on food are still relevant today, as perhaps is his description of the ideal cook, who

> must be cleanly both in body and garments, she must have a quick eye, a curious nose, a perfect taste, and a ready care (she must not be butter-fingered, sweete-toothed, nor faint-hearted;) for, the first will

let everything fall, the second will consume what it should increase, and the last will loose time with too much niceness.

If such were the standards of the best seventeenth-century cooks, it is not surprising that people thought it worth while to visit Mrs Woolley for instruction, or to find well-trained servants. Mrs Woolley's standards are worth remembering today, just as her recipes themselves are.

In adapting the recipes for modern enjoyment, I have been inspired by the spirit behind them, by the wide range of herbs and spices employed, for instance, or the strikingly different and interesting combinations of fruit with meat or fish. I hope that, even if you don't actually cook any of the particular dishes described in this book, you may be tempted, after reading it, to try a different range of flavours from usual. I don't expect anyone to follow my recipes exactly, if they can think of a different or better way, any more than I tried exactly to follow the originals. As Mrs Woolley herself says, in *The Gentlewoman's Companion*:

> I have given you an Essay, or small pattern of Cookery, not desiring to tye you too strictly to the observation of those rules I have here laid for your imitation; but desire to give your fancy all convenient liberty in conceiving what you may find amiss herein.

The task of transforming Mrs Woolley's 'receipts' into modern recipes was not always easy. The idea of organising recipes into lists of ingredients, with amounts of each, followed by a detailed 'method', was unknown in her time, and anything like the almost scientific precision often encountered in today's elaborate cookery books did not appear until well into the eighteenth century. Mrs Woolley and her contemporaries are not generally consistent in such matters: some of her recipes give quite exact quantities, such as the ones for sack possets, while others have an almost wilfully vague air, sometimes giving an impression of prodigal luxury. 'Scald three or four chickens,' she says at the start of a recipe for 'Fricacie of Chickens', or, in a recipe for stewing a pig, 'Take a large Pig to the fire'. (There is no mention of *how* one was supposed to get it there; presumably the servants helped.)

Naturally, I have tended to reduce quantities to suit the smaller numbers of people commonly present at dinner these days – all the recipes are intended for four people unless otherwise stated – but I have also had to make up my own mind about what the finished dishes should actually taste like, and how they should be presented. For instance, I have adapted a recipe for a whole rump of beef for steaks, and shoulders of lamb for chops. Once again, I would like to emphasize that these are my own interpretations, and should not be taken as gospel: the kitchen is, after all, a place for creation, not repetition.

One thing which I have not been able to adapt is the imbalance between different kinds of dishes. A casual glance at the contents page will show that there are far more recipes for meat dishes and desserts than anything else. This reflects not just the contents of Mrs Woolley's own books, but also to a great extent the archetypal dietary proclivities of the seventeenth century. It must be confessed that this is not a book for those who are on a diet; it reflects the tastes of an age in which nutritional science was in its infancy, but hearty enjoyment of good, natural ingredients – in large amounts, if possible – was the rule. Nevertheless, there are many recipes for fish, vegetables and white meats to try, so I hope that everyone will find something to his or her taste.

A brief note on the ingredients and methods used in the recipes may be thought useful. A general rule which nowadays might be regarded as Utopian is that given by Gervase Markham, who maintained that a good cook's ingredients should 'proceed more from the provision of her own yarde, then the furniture of the markets'. Those cooks who are also gardeners are certainly well placed to obtain fresh herbs, choice vegetables and fruit, perhaps even free-range eggs. However, those of us who have to buy all, or nearly all, of our ingredients, can still insist on high-quality, natural materials.

For reasons of authenticity and flavour, when adapting Mrs Woolley's recipes, I have used natural and unrefined products wherever possible: raw cane sugar, wholemeal flour, free-range eggs and poultry, and so on. With the growing interest in a healthy diet and concern for the conditions both of the animals which are bred for food, and of those who eat them, there has been a huge increase in the availability of such products. It is interesting to note that, even in the comparatively short time in which I've been preparing this book, free-range poultry, fresh herbs and organically grown vegetables have become much commoner in supermarkets, rather than being confined to 'health shops' and the more exclusive delicatessens. Being able to cook with such ingredients makes an enormous difference to the quality of these recipes, and of course they are much closer to the materials which Mrs Woolley herself would have used.

A good example of the way our eating habits are to some extent coming full circle is with flour. Before the invention, in the nineteenth century, of steam mills, even the finest white wheaten

flour was 'whole', because no machinery existed to crush the wheat
germ and reveal the white flour within. Bread was made with a
variety of flours, ranging from the finest manchet to coarse flour
made from rye or even oats. White wheaten bread, at the top of the
scale, was especially favoured in London. There is a story that some
Dutch sailors staying there towards the end of the century,
complained that their white bread was too bland, compared with
that which they ate at home. This, the most expensive bread, was
only 'white' compared to cheaper kinds, and nothing like as white as
today's. It was made from the best wheat, ground and sifted as much
as possible, but still contained the natural goodness which modern
methods remove. The whiteness of bread was a mark of its quality, a
fact which led to twentieth-century bakers making their bread
whiter-than-white, by bleaching the flour and other methods.
Recently the idea that the best bread is the whitest has been losing
favour, and wholemeal bread – despised in the past, along with other
brown bread, as inferior – has come back into fashion.

It would be wrong to imagine that all food was unrefined in the
seventeenth century. We know from Mrs Woolley herself that white
sugar was made by dyeing raw sugar with lime. Refined foods are
worth avoiding now on grounds of flavour as well as health –
jumbals, for instance, lose most of their attractivness if made with
white flour and white sugar, caramel-dyed or otherwise, instead of
wholemeal flour and raw, rich, dark muscovado. As for free-range
eggs, I have usually found them to have much yellower yolks, and
finer rising properties than the battery-produced variety. The
questions of flavour and authenticity are of course related. Mrs
Woolley wrote her recipes for the ingredients she knew, and if we
make them with pale imitations, we can't expect equally good
results. Therefore when a recipe says 'flour' or 'sugar', it *always*
means the unrefined kind.

In the matter of herbs, the seventeenth century cooks were luckier
than us, usually having at their disposal either a well-stocked herb
garden or a profusion of wild herbs, or both. Thomas Tusser, in his
Hundreth Good Pointes of Husbandrie (1557), gives a list of some
three hundred 'common' herbs, and ends it by saying: 'Who more
would have, must fields go crave.' Not only did cooks have access to
many herbs which have almost died out now, they could also use
fresh herbs to a far greater extent. Anyone who has ever had a
baytree, for instance, will know the advantages of the fresh leaf over
the dried. In all the recipes I have specified fresh herbs, and it is
worth trying to find them whenever possible. Otherwise I have
given quantities for dried herbs as an alternative.

A different problem is that of highly unusual ingredients. When Mrs Woolley specified something which I'd never seen, or even heard of, I either hunted down the original or used what I thought was an acceptable substitute. Sometimes it has been impossible to obtain the item. For instance, herbs such as clary, or samphire, formerly much used for preserving, seem to have vanished for ever, at least in my part of the world, though I believe the latter can be bought in season at the Chelsea Farmer's Market in Sydney St, London. (I'm indebted to Hilary Spurling's fascinating *Elinor Fettiplace's Receipt Book* for this information.) This has meant my leaving out some recipes, not without regret, but I decided that others, in which the missing ingredient was not the most important flavouring, could be included, as for instance 'Smoored Chicken'. (page 73) (If you are a country dweller, and adept at finding wild herbs, you may have more success in tracking down ingredients than I did.)

Other unusual ingredients can often be manufactured reasonably well. The most important of these is verjuice, a sharp flavouring made from the juice of sour fruit and widely used in the seventeenth century. It was generally made from either crab-apples or sour grapes, and, if you do not have access to crab-apples, and cannot find crab-apple juice commercially, a mixture of two parts lemon juice to one of apple juice provides a good alternative. To save repeating myself in the recipes, I only specify amounts of 'made' verjuice, and I always mean apple-based juice.

MEAT

IT is a common belief that, whatever the poverty of the English, they have always eaten far more meat than the inhabitants of the Continent. 'The Roast Beef of Old England' has often been compared to the fare of the Continent, perhaps most famously by Thackeray, who explains to his English readers why they are taller and stronger than the French: 'The Frenchman has after his soup a dish of vegetables, where you have one of meat.' Foreign travellers remarked on the amount of meat eaten by the British, and in the late autumn, because there was little or no winter feed for the cattle, the large-scale slaughtering of livestock meant there *was* plenty of fresh meat around, even though a lot of it was salted down for the long winter months. (Hence the popularity of traditional English dishes like pea and ham soup, made from dried peas and home-cured ham.)

However, this large intake of meat was confined to those who could afford it, and when it was in season. In 1691 the Rev. Richard Baxter described a poor man's family who ate meat just once a week, and then only a piece of hanged bacon 'enough to trie the stomach of an ostridge'. Salted meat was the only meat many people ever ate, and pork was the commonest as pigs could be fed on almost anything. Salted or smoked, they were made to last the whole winter. (Readers of Flora Thomson's *Lark Rise to Candleford* will remember that much the same pig-based domestic economy was being practised in rural Oxfordshire two hundred years later.) Pigs might also provide extra cash too, as their piglets could be sold at market. At the higher levels of society, it is true, a lot of meat was eaten, and everyone who lived in the large country houses of the wealthy would expect to eat meat regularly. Either the estate's farms would provide it, or carcasses would be bought in: the Earl of Bedford was paying 1/8d (8p) a stone for beef during the Civil War.

Usually, meat would be roasted on spits in front of those great open fires which look picturesque to the modern eye, but which claimed almost as many women's lives as did childbirth. It is impossible to recapture now the flavour of those whole pigs or saddles of mutton, turned for hours by the labour of animals in treadmills, and basted continuously with wine and the juice from the meat until a hard crisp coating was formed. Other ways of cooking included 'broiling', where steaks of meat were either cooked on a gridiron set over the coals, or impaled on what look like spiked firescreens held up to the fire, with the juices collected in a tray below to make the sauce. Whole small joints might be boiled long and slow in cauldrons suspended by chains above the fire, while fricassees would be cooked in smaller stewpans, and pies and pasties baked in the bread oven.

All this required an exact knowledge of the heating properties of the fuel, which varied from region to region, giving a local character to various dishes. Cornish cooking, for instance, dependent to a large extent on slow-burning peat, produced baked meats like pasties, and clotted cream, both of which need reliable, slow heat, unlike the fiery heat given out by wood and coal fires. Of course, the ovens could be erratic too, so that cooks of the time had to become adept at putting different breads, pies, and cakes into the oven in the right sequence: there are many instructions in the seventeenth and eighteenth centuries to bake a particular dish 'when the bread is drawn', and the oven had cooled a little from its zenith. I've adapted the following recipes with an eye to the conveniences of the modern kitchen, for which, having read so much about those of three hundred years ago, I am even more thankful than usual.

BEEF

Most of my selection of Mrs Woolley's beef recipes are rich, highly flavoured stews at which she excels, but I've also included two other dishes for grilled and fried beef. Incidentally, I've followed Mrs Woolley's and my own preference in cooking the casseroles on top of the stove, but it's perfectly possible to make them in the oven, if you prefer.

Beef Stew with Herbs and Nuts
A Hash of Beef

This rich, aromatic casserole, especially good on winter evenings, goes well with baked potatoes, and really deserves a more glamorous title than 'hash'. For Mrs Woolley and her contemporaries, a 'hash' was simply a dish in which the meat was chopped up, rather than being roasted or stewed in whole joints – the word did not have the denigratory connotations it has nowadays. (It derives from the French *hacher*, to cut up.) Mrs Woolley's recipe explains how small the meat should be chopped:

> *Cut your Beef, fat and lean, into Gobbets, as big as a Pullets Egg, and put them into a pot or Pipkin with some Carrots cut into pieces as big as a Walnut . . .*

These are very exact measurements for a cook used to handling such things every day, and to whom measurements in inches might be irrelevant. Likewise, in some early cookery books, one is told to boil food for as long as it takes to say the Lord's Prayer, rather than for a specific number of minutes. I've also adapted Mrs Woolley's stewing method to more modern tastes by frying the vegetables and meat first; she simply puts everything in the pan with 'as much water and wine as will cover them, let them thus stew three hours'. The addition of the lemon as a final touch was suggested by another of Mrs Woolley's long list of 'hashes'.

1½lb/675g stewing or braising steak cut into 1in/ 2cm squares	½pt/300ml red wine
	½pt/300ml beef stock
3 tablespoons vegetable oil	1 tablespoon each of fresh chopped tarragon,
10 pickling onions	marjoram, parsley and
3 parsnips, chopped	thyme
3 carrots, chopped	2oz/50g chestnuts or almonds
½ nutmeg, freshly grated	Salt and pepper to taste
3 large blades of mace	A lemon, peeled and sliced

Heat the oil in a large saucepan and gently fry the vegetables until lightly browned. Add the meat and cook, stirring, until it is brown all over, then add the remaining ingredients. Bring to the boil, cover and simmer for 2½–3 hours or until the meat and roots are tender. Add half the lemon slices to the stew about 30 minutes before the end of the cooking time, to let their flavour infuse – you can remove them before serving. Garnish the finished dish with the remainder.
    Serves 4

This is another of Mrs Woolley's rich stews, similar to the previous recipe but with the addition of more fruit and vegetables. The 'French' label may have been an attempt to capitalize on the contemporary fashion for all things French. I'm not convinced that there is really anything French about it.

Beef Casserole with Grapes or Gooseberries
To Stew Beef in Goggets, the French Fashion

The original recipe explains which cuts of beef to use, and also shows how elaborately Mrs Woolley garnished her dishes:

> Take a Flank of Beef, or any part but the Leg, cut it into slices, or Gobbets as big as Pullet's-Eggs, with some Gobbets of Fat, and boyl it in a Pot or Pipkin with some fair spring-water . . . Garnish it with Grapes, Barberries, or Gooseberries: Or else use Spices, the bottoms of boyled Artichoaks put into beaten Butter, and grated Nutmeg, garnished with barberries.

The stipulation of spring-water is a reminder that one had to be careful about the water-supply at this period, even in the country, where the local stream might easily become contaminated. When 'fair' water was not available, other cooking liquids were often used – hence the popularity of wine and rosewater in cooking. In adapting this recipe, I was rather spoilt for choice of garnish. The original would have looked very impressive: the great dish of beef, surrounded by heaps of glistening, brightly coloured barberries or grapes, carried in to the diners. I chose grapes or gooseberries, as being easy to obtain in season and complimenting the flavour of the meat very well.

The spinach and sorrel are used here as herbs, like the rest; indeed, Mrs Woolley always refers to spinach, lettuce, etc, as herbs, as distinct from roots such as carrots and parsnips. The point was made by an earlier writer that the roots of parsley contained more goodness than the leaves, and I have seen an Elizabethan recipe which specifies parsley and fennel *roots*, rather than leaves. If you cannot get hold of sorrel, use two handfuls of spinach and add the juice of half a lemon with it. This isn't an exact substitute, though, and it really is worth trying to find sorrel – it's very easy to grow and very hardy once established.

1½lb/675g stewing or
    braising steak
2 large onions, roughly
    chopped
2 tablespoons sunflower oil
3 blades of mace
About 1 tablespoon each of
    fresh chopped thyme,
    parsley, marjoram and
    savory, or 2 teaspoons each
    of dried
Salt and pepper to taste

4oz/100g red or black grapes,
    or gently cooked
    gooseberries
2 parsnips, chopped
2 turnips, chopped
2 large carrots, chopped
4 cloves
½pt/300ml red wine
¼pt/150ml beef stock
A handful each of spinach and
    sorrel, washed, trimmed
    and chopped

Heat the oil in a large saucepan, fry the onions until lightly
browned, then add the beef and cook quickly until browned all
over. Stir in the root vegetables,.herbs (except for the spinach
and sorrel) and spice, cook for a minute then pour in the wine
and stock. Season to taste, bring to the boil, then cover and
simmer, stirring occasionally, for 2½–3 hours, or until the meat
is tender. If it becomes too dry, add a little more stock or wine.

Stir the chopped spinach and sorrel into the stew about 10
minutes before the end of the cooking time – this final touch
gives the dish its unusual tang.

Serve with baked or mashed potatoes, or rice, and serve the
grapes or gooseberries in a separate dish.

Serves 4.

The next recipe stands out among Mrs Woolley's stews as being
made with spices, rather than the more usual herbs. Perhaps this
difference accounts for the dish being *à la mode*.

Beef Stewed with Spices
Beef A-la-mode

The original recipe is one of Mrs Woolley's simpler ones, and short
enough to quote in full:

> Cut some Buttock-beef a quarter of an inch thick and lard it with
> Bacon, having hackt it before a little with the back of your knife, then

stew it in a Pipkin with some gravy, Claret-wine, and strong Broth,
Cloves, Mace, Pepper, Cinnamon and Salt; being tender stewed, serve
it on French-bread sippets.

The result is quite strong, with a flavour unlike Mrs Woolley's other
stews, which may take a little getting used to – especially, perhaps, the
cinnamon and cloves, which the modern cook associates more with
puddings than stews. I've replaced her 'buttock-beef' with a good
tender braising steak, though if you can afford the extravagance, rump
steak makes a wonderful dish. I use smoked streaky bacon, as it's not
only very authentic – smoking was one of the standard methods for
preserving bacon – but adds a dark, smokey flavour to the stew. The
'gravy' mentioned in the original recipe is not the same as modern
gravy; it was a very rich, reduced stock, produced from the large range
of marrow-bones and carcasses available in the seventeenth-century
kitchen, but not today. Generally, I replace it with strong, home-made
meat stock, and increase the ratio of wine to stock.

1½lb/675g stewing steak, cubed	*½pt/300ml red wine*
	4 cloves
4oz/100g streaky bacon, rind removed	*3 blades of mace*
	3 teaspoons cinnamon
1 tablespoon oil for frying	*Salt and pepper to taste*
¼pt/150ml good beef stock	

Heat a little oil in a saucepan. Cut the bacon into short strips
and gently fry until the fat is transparent, but not crisp. Add the
beef and cook quickly until browned all over. Add the spices,
stir and cook for a minute, then pour on the wine and stock.
Season to taste, bring to the boil, then lower the heat, cover and
simmer gently for up to an hour, depending on the quality of the
meat. A good stewing steak might only need 30–40 minutes.

If the stew needs any more liquid during cooking, add a little
more wine, but don't let it get too runny: the sauce should coat
the meat, rather than the meat swim in the sauce.

Serves 4.

The next beef casserole is perhaps even more out of the way. I cannot
think of a common modern equivalent in English cooking, but the
German *Sauerbraten* is a possible analogy to this vinegar-flavoured
stew.

Beef Stewed with Red Wine and Vinegar
To stew a Rump of Beef

This is a dish with an unusual and very strong flavour. Originally it was for a whole rump of beef, cooked in 'three pints of Elder-Vinegar, and three pints of Water', which is a fairly typical quantity for Mrs Woolley's recipes. Although in this version I have made it with rump or stewing steak as a casserole, a similar method could be tried on a pot-roast joint, laid 'in the Pipkin with the fat side downward'. Instead of the water and vinegar, I use a mixture of red wine (preferably home-made elderberry wine, for the 'elder' flavour) and red-wine vinegar. If you don't have elderberry wine, use a well-flavoured, fruity red, such as Bulgarian Cabernet Sauvignon. Finding the right proportions of wine to vinegar is largely a matter of trial and error, depending on personal taste; I use about half and half. A touch of dark muscovado sugar adds colour and helps soften the sharpness a little.

1½lb/675g stewing or rump steak, cut into 1in/2cm squares	6fl oz/175ml elderberry wine
	6fl oz/175ml red wine vinegar
	2–3 sprigs of rosemary
2 large onions, roughly chopped	Salt and pepper to taste
Butter for frying	1 dessertspoon dark muscovado sugar (optional)
1 nutmeg	

Melt the butter in a large saucepan, brown the meat quickly and remove. Add a little more butter if necessary and fry the onions for 3–4 minutes. Grate on the nutmeg and stir well. Allow to cook for a minute, then return the beef to the pan, add the rosemary and pour in the wine and vinegar. Bring to the boil, then lower the heat to a simmer, season to taste and cook for about two hours, or less if you use rump steak.

Check the flavour – don't worry if the bouquet is a little eye-watering, as the vinegar, being highly volatile, smells much stronger than it tastes. Add the sugar if you feel you need it, stirring well to ensure that it dissolves.

Serves 4.

Back to more familiar territory with this succulent variation on the ever-popular grilled steak, which, along with prawn cocktail and black forest gâteau, has been part of Britain's favourite restaurant menu for years. This method takes it out of its usual rut.

Marinaded Grilled Steak
Beef Carbonadoed

Although Mrs Woolley's name for this dish sounds similar to the French *carbonade*, there is no similarity between the way they are prepared. In the seventeenth century, a *carbonado* was a dish of meat broiled over the coals – the word comes from the Spanish for charcoal. The most authentic way of making carbonadoed beef would be on a charcoal barbeque, which uses almost exactly the same method of cooking as Mrs Woolley's fire. The original recipe gives a clear picture of one of the period's standard methods of cooking:

> *Steep your beef in Claret-wine, Salt, Pepper and Nutmeg, then broil it on the Embers over a temperate and unsmoaky fire, in the mean while boil up the liquor wherein it was steeped; and serve it for sauce, with beaten Butter.*

This is a simple recipe, which, apart from the marinading, does not take long to prepare. It makes an interesting variation on grilled steak.

Four 6–8oz/175–225g rump or	*Salt and pepper*
sirloin steaks	*A whole nutmeg*
½pt/300ml red wine	*2oz/50g butter*
	Beef stock (optional)

Tenderize the meat with a meat hammer or the back of a heavy knife. Grate the nutmeg on to both sides of each steak, and then season them well with salt and pepper. Lay them in a flat dish and pour on enough wine to completely cover them. Cover the dish and leave to marinate, preferably in the refrigerator, for at least 2 hours – the longer the better, as the immersion not only flavours the meat but tenderizes it. After marination, take the steaks from the dish, smear a little butter on them and grill for 8–10 minutes, according to taste.

Meanwhile, add a little stock to reduce the strength of the marinade and reduce it by boiling in a small saucepan until it begins to thicken. Then lower the heat and stir in the remaining butter.

When the steaks are cooked, place them on a serving dish, add the juice from the grillpan to the sauce, stir well and pour over the steaks. Alternatively, you can make the sauce before grilling the steaks, then re-heat it with the juices from the grillpan before serving.
Serves 4.

This next recipe is perhaps the nearest – except for oysters – Mrs Woolley gets to fast food – a kind of seventeenth-century meatcake or hamburger.

Mrs Woolley's Hamburgers
A Dish of Meat with Herbs

The recipe is rather vague in the original, but I decided to try it out because I was immediately attracted by the remarkable range of ingredients:

Take Sives [chives], Parsley, Thyme, Marjoram, & Roast three or four Eggs hard, and a quantity of Mutton-suet, Beef, or Lamb, chop them fine all together, and season it with Cloves, Mace, Ginger, Sugar, and Cinnamon, and a little salt; then Fry them with a little sweet butter.

Rather than fry the mixture loose, as it were, I thought the best way to cook the meat was to form it in into 'burgers'. The result is much more appetising than the limp nonentities offered up by the average High-Street Burgo-Bland. I also decided to leave out the suet and the sugar – I didn't find that they really did anything for the flavour, but some people might like to try adding two teaspoonfuls of each to the mixture. Steak mince is very good for this dish, though as Mrs Woolley says, you can use lamb if you like.

1lb/450g very lean minced beef
3 tablespoons mixed fresh chives, parsley, marjoram and thyme, finely chopped, or 4 teaspoons dried
2 eggs, hardboiled, shelled and chopped

1 teaspoon each of ground mace, ginger, sugar and cinnamon
A pinch of ground cloves
Salt and pepper
1 egg, beaten (optional)
2oz/50g butter for frying

Mix all the ingredients together, seasoning to taste. Form the mixture into burgers – use the beaten egg to bind them if you find that they do not stay together. Melt the butter in a frying pan and cook the 'hamburgers' over a moderate heat for 5–6 minutes each side, or until no juice runs out when you prod them with the point of a knife or skewer.
Serves 4.

LAMB

Almost all the recipes in this section were originally for mutton. It was traditional in England to kill the beast later in the season, rather than in the spring, when they were smaller and consequently worth less. The stronger flavour of mutton – which was significantly different to that of lamb – was preferred, and only a handful of Mrs Woolley's recipes specify lamb. Nowadays the fashion has completely reversed, and it is difficult to obtain mutton in the shops, though, with an interesting historical irony, this very traditional English food can be bought in halal butchers. Seventeenth-century cooks could never have foreseen that a commonplace of their tables would be more familiar in the Muslim community, and that saddles of mutton, once an essential part of the English diet, are only sighted now at restaurants like Simpson's-in-the-Strand.

Making the following dishes with lamb means that they cannot be regarded as replicas of Restoration food. However, the recipes are intended to be personal re-creations, not historical reconstructions.

Roast Leg of Lamb
To roast a Legg of Mutton

I call this *roast* lamb, but Mrs Woolley would not recognise the modern oven-baking of meat as being anything of the sort, as it's not cooked on a spit. That in itself means the finished joint was different in flavour and texture from anything produced today, a difference increased by the fact that the cooks of the past roasted much larger joints, which tasted different because they took that much longer to cook. In adapting the recipe I've borne in mind these differences, but I've also attempted to incorporate one or two features of seventeenth-century spit-roasting, most importantly the process of basting with wine and coating in flour, which produced the characteristic crisp top layer. In Mrs Woolley's kitchen, a menial would 'dredge the legg with flower', and baste it with claret and the juices collected in the pan under the spit almost continually during the cooking. This isn't practical nowadays, but I hope the modern version gives some idea of the method.

A leg of lamb (3lb/1.5kg approx)	*2 teaspoons dried ginger*
12 cloves	*Verjuice made with half a lemon*
1oz/25g lard or butter	*2 teaspoons capers, finely chopped*
6fl oz/170ml red wine	
Two or three sprigs each of fresh parsley, thyme and rosemary finely chopped, or 2 teaspoons each, dried	*2oz/50g butter*
	1 hard-boiled egg yolk
	Pepper and salt

Preheat the oven to Gas Mark 8/230°C/450°F. Reserve half the wine for the sauce.

Smear the lard or butter over the joint. Make a few incisions in the meat and stick the cloves in them. Put on to a rack in a roasting pan and roast for 15 minutes, then turn the oven down to gas Mark 4/180°C/350°F. Take the joint out, lightly dust it with flour and pour over a couple of tablespoons of the wine. Return it to the oven and roast for about 30 minutes per pound. Repeat the basting and flouring every 20–30 minutes – baste it with the juices in the roasting tin as well.

After about an hour's cooking at the lower temperature, take out the joint and cut off about four very thin slices of lean meat and return the joint to the oven. Chop the slices as finely as possible, until they are almost paste-like. Melt the butter in a small saucepan and add the meat, herbs, capers and ginger. Stir well, then add the verjuice and reserved wine. Let the mixture simmer for 15 minutes, then take a tablespoon of the liquid and mash it up with the egg yolk. Return the resulting liaison to the saucepan and mix thoroughly. Season to taste and transfer to a warm sauceboat. As a luxurious alternative, you can thicken the sauce with a tablespoon of double cream – not historically authentic, but very good.

Serves 5–6.

My title for the next dish may conjure up visions of *nouvelle cuisine*, but it's really only a way of amalgamating two different recipes, one for lamb with red wine sauce, and the other for sorrel sauce, which I found went well together.

Grilled Lamb Steaks with Two Sauces
To Carbonado Mutton

This is a very simple recipe for 'carbonadoed', ie grilled, lamb. Like the 'carbonadoed' beef on page 43, it is a good recipe for cooking on a barbecue. I use leg of lamb steaks, though it is also good with chops – accompanied by a hot red wine sauce and a sorrel relish, which Mrs Woolley calls green sauce. The hot sauce is also good with beef, and is quite simple to make:

> *Claret-wine boyled up with two Onions, a little Camphire and Capers, with a little Gravey, Garnish'd with Limons.*

I couldn't find any samphire (though see page 35), but the sauce works well enough without it. I've also added some sugar, which helps the flavour.

4 steaks cut from a leg of lamb	1 lemon
1 tablespoon fresh thyme, finely chopped	Nutmeg for grating Butter

For the sauces:

(1)	2oz/50g butter for frying	(2)	1oz/25g fresh sorrel, washed and trimmed
	2 onions, finely chopped		½ small eating apple, finely grated
	6 teaspoons capers, chopped		2 teaspoons raw cane sugar
	¾pt/450ml red wine		1 tablespoon cider vinegar
	1 dessertspoon muscovado sugar		

To make the first sauce, melt the butter in a small saucepan and sweat the onions, covered, over a low heat for about 15 minutes, until they are soft. Then add the capers, cook for another minute, and pour on the wine. Cook over a brisk heat, uncovered, adding sugar to taste, for about another 10 minutes, or until the wine has reduced by about a quarter.

For the second, chop the sorrel as finely as possible, then mix together with the apple. Dissolve the sugar in the vinegar, then blend with the apple and sorrel. (If you're making larger quantities, use a liquidizer.) Put the sauce into a small bowl for serving. (Mrs Woolley tells the reader to 'put it into Saucers', a reminder of their original use.)

Tenderize the steaks with the back of a heavy knife (just as good as a meat hammer); this helps flatten them too, which means it's easier to cook them thoroughly. Arrange them on the grill, sprinkle with thyme, liberally grate the nutmeg over them and season with pepper and salt. Put a dab of butter on each and cook under a moderate grill for about 5–6 minutes each side.

When they are ready, re-heat the red wine sauce and transfer to a warm sauceboat. Arrange the steaks on a warmed serving dish and garnish them with the lemon quarters for added zest. The same herbs, and the same sauces, can be used very well with roast leg or shoulder of lamb.

Serves 4.

The fact that Mrs Woolley used steaks of mutton in the next recipe, rather than chops, as would be more likely today, is interesting. Perhaps diners of the period liked the extra meat one finds on a steak, as compared to a chop. Of course, it reflects the fact that she did not buy her meat ready-dressed, but could buy a whole leg (or indeed, a whole side) of mutton, and cut it up as she liked.

Lamb Steaks Sautéed with Lemon
To Smoor Steaks of Mutton

'To smoor' is a verb meaning 'smother', and suggests meat cooked in a sauce. In Mrs Woolley's 'smoored' recipes, the sauce usually tends to be quite sharp, including white wine, herbs and lemon or crab-apple juice. This particular dish uses slices from a leg of mutton, for which boned leg of lamb steaks make a good and easily available substitute. If you like, the steaks can be beaten with a meat-tenderizer or the back of a heavy knife before frying, which helps them to cook evenly and thoroughly. Some people may prefer lamb chops, as having more flavour, but I find these are less easy to fry satisfactorily.

The original recipe suggests frying the meat first 'in White-wine and a little Salt, a bundle of Herbs, and a little Limon peel', then transferring it to another pan for further frying in butter, with parsley and more lemon. To save time and washing up, I've combined the two operations – it doesn't seem to make any difference to the taste.

4½in/11·5cm steaks cut from a leg of lamb	4oz/100g fresh cranberries or 1 lemon, sliced
2oz/50g butter for frying	½pt/300ml white wine
1 tablespoon each of fresh rosemary, thyme and parsley, chopped	1 lemon, peeled Salt and pepper

Melt the butter in a frying pan and sauté the steaks gently until they are coloured on both sides.

Meanwhile finely chop the lemon peel and slice the lemon. Pour the wine into the meat and add the herbs, lemon peel and sliced lemon. Season well, then bring to the boil and simmer for 20–30 minutes or until the meat is tender.

Transfer the meat to a dish and keep hot while reducing the sauce over high heat. If desired, the sauce can be strained over the meat, giving it the flavour of herbs and lemon without any bits in it. This is purely a matter of taste.

Garnish the dish with either another lemon, thinly sliced, or cranberries (as a substitute for barberries). If you can't get fresh cranberries, which tend to be imported from Italy and sold in the Christmas season, serve cranberry sauce.

Serves 4.

This next dish is a rare example of Mrs Woolley using lamb, rather than mutton – another example is the recipe for lamb pies on page 52. Lamb was more expensive than mutton, of course, and perhaps Mrs Woolley thought it was therefore to be rationed.

Braised Lamb with Fruit
To stew a Leg of Lamb

Although Mrs Woolley specifies leg of lamb, I've made this very successfully with shoulder, which can often be bought ready-chopped for stewing, as braising lamb. The original recipe throws an interesting sidelight on cooking methods and ingredients: you season the lamb with salt and nutmeg, then

> *put it into your stewing-pan . . . with as much butter as will stew it . . . when it is stewed, make a Caudle with the Yolks of two or three Eggs, and some Wine-Vinegar and Sugar beaten together . . .*

It is perhaps surprising to see meat being stewed, rather than fried, in butter, but in fact butter was used extensively in cookery at this period, especially to tenderize meat, which was tougher than that available today. Hence its presence in this recipe. Butter was comparatively cheap, but its use was mostly confined to cooking – it was not eaten raw, with bread, because it had a very strong flavour due to the heavy salting which was the only method of preservation. To suit modern tastes, I've reduced the amount of butter and substituted white wine. The thickening is also typical – a caudle generally meant a kind of hot wine drink mixed with gruel, but here is used to mean a liaison. If you prefer, it can be made with lemon juice, but it's very good with a lightly-flavoured white wine vinegar.

1½lb/675g lean shoulder of lamb, cut into small cubes	*2oz/50g raisins*
	2oz/50g currants
1 nutmeg, grated	*6 floz/175ml white wine*
Salt and pepper	*2 egg yolks*
4oz/100g butter	*1 tablespoon white wine*
4oz/100g gooseberries or white grapes	*vinegar*

Coat the meat all over with the grated nutmeg and season well with salt and pepper. Melt the butter in a saucepan and add the meat. Fry for a few minutes, stirring frequently until the meat is well browned all over. Add the fruit and the wine, lower the heat and simmer for 40–45 minutes, or until the lamb is very tender.

Beat the egg yolks and vinegar together and, when the meat is ready, gradually stir in the caudle. Cook for another couple of minutes, stirring constantly, then pile into a heated serving dish and serve immediately.

Serves 4–5.

Here is another recipe in which meat is cooked with dried fruit. I think it is this tradition of mixing the two which re-appears, or is continued, in the classic Anglo-Indian curry, with its raisins and sultanas. Certainly it was not introduced to British cooking from India, as all these recipes have shown, but it seems to have become associated with Indian food anyway. Indian food in Britain does not seem to be such a modern innovation, incidentally; the word curry, from a Tamil word meaning a sauce or relish, entered the language in the sixteenth century.

Meatballs made with Lamb
To make balls of veal or mutton

I make these with lamb, but the original suggests an alternative:

> *Take a leg of mutton or fillet of veal, mince it small, with penyroial and parsley, then mingle it with a little grated bread and currans, and two eggs well beaten; season them with cloves, mace, pepper and salt; make them like tennis balls, and crush them together with your hands . . .*

Mincing a whole fillet of veal would be a bit extravagant these days, and perhaps also in the seventeenth century, when one could pay ninepence just for a shoulder – not a sum that everyone could afford. If your butcher will mince some leg of lamb, it will do very well. Otherwise, use the leanest minced lamb you can find, as too much fat makes the sauce greasy and unpleasant.

I haven't come across fresh pennyroyal, a little-known but fragrant herb, but it should be possible to find it dried. If not, use thyme. The stock should be home-made, and well skimmed of fat.

2lb/900g minced lamb	4oz/100g wholemeal
2 tablespoons finely chopped	breadcrumbs
fresh parsley	4oz/100g currants
2 teaspoons dried pennyroyal	A pinch of cloves
or 1 tablespoon fresh, if you	2 teaspoons ground mace
can get it	1–2 egg yolks
Pepper and salt	3/4pt/450ml chicken or lamb
Butter for frying	stock

Mix together the meat, breadcrumbs, herbs, spices, egg yolk and half the currants. Season well and form into little balls – Mrs Woolley's instruction to 'make them like tennis balls, and crush them together with your hands' shows the best method. She was referring to the balls used for real tennis, much smaller than those used for modern lawn tennis. This recipe should make about 8–10 reasonably substantial balls.

Melt the butter in a large saucepan, and brown the balls all over. Add enough stock to cover, with the rest of the currants, and cook for about 20 minutes on a moderate heat, so the liquid bubbles gently rather than boils.

Serves 4.

This is the other recipe I've included from Mrs Woolley's very small selection of ways to cook lamb, as opposed to mutton. Once again, it includes the familiar dried fruit.

Lamb Pies
To make a Lamb Pye

I don't have any hard evidence as to which kind of pastry Mrs Woolley used in this recipe – usually she only mentions the pastry when she uses puff pastry. However, I decided that these lamb pies could be made as raised pies with a hot-water crust, as this was the commonest type of pastry well into the next century. However, I've cheated slightly by making the crust a little richer than usual. It has the advantage that it can be made very quickly, and of course the finished product looks very impressive.

The quantities below make four 4in/10cm pies, or one very big one. The smaller ones are easier to make, as for the larger one a proper hinged pie mould is required.

For the pastry:
12oz/340g wholemeal flour   *⅓pt/200ml milk*
1 teaspoon salt   *4oz/100g lard or vegetable fat*
     Egg yolk and milk for the
        glaze

For the filling:
8oz/225g lamb shoulder   *2 cloves, crushed*
1oz/25g currants   *Salt to taste*
1oz/25g raisins   *An egg yolk lightly beaten*

1oz/25g butter
2 teaspoons freshly grated nutmeg
1 teaspoon ground mace

with 1 dessertspoon vinegar or lemon juice

Chop the lamb into fairly small pieces, but don't mince it. Mix it thoroughly with the dried fruit, butter and spices, season to taste and stir in the egg mixture.

To make the pastry, sift the flour and salt into a mixing bowl. Put the milk and fat into a saucepan and bring just to the boil, then make a well in the centre of the flour and pour in the liquid. Mix to a soft dough – add a little extra hot water if necessary. Knead quickly, keeping the pastry warm, as it hardens when it cools down.

Reserve about a third of the pastry, and divide the rest into four. Roll the pieces into balls, and form them into cases, using the base of a tumbler (or something similar) lightly floured, as a mould, or working the paste with your fingers. Put the cases on to a greased baking sheet and fill them with the meat mixture. Roll out the remaining pastry for the lids, moisten the edges of the pie cases with a little milk to ensure that the pies will be properly sealed and put on the lids. Cut a slit in the top of each pie and brush with egg yolk beaten in a little milk.

Bake in a fairly hot oven (Gas Mark 7/220°C/425°F) for about 10 minutes, then lower the heat to Gas Mark 5/190°C/375°F and continue cooking for another 30 minutes. These can be eaten hot, in which case allow them to stand for a few minutes before serving, or cold.

Serves 4.

PORK AND VEAL

I've brought the recipes for pork and veal together because I've found that they are largely interchangeable, and indeed, Mrs Woolley frequently specifies two or three different types of meat which are suitable for a particular recipe.

Pork was certainly a more traditional English food, especially among the poorer classes, as a pig could be kept in a comparatively confined space and fed on almost anything. Furthermore, there was little waste on a pig; everything, including the trotters and head, could be eaten somehow. Veal tended (then and now) to be the preserve of the well-off. On the whole, English farmers bred cattle for beef rather than veal, as they bred sheep for mutton rather than lamb. Veal was regarded as a French taste, and so became more fashionable as French influence increased.

Many people nowadays object to eating veal on humanitarian grounds because of the way calves are reared, so it's worth making it clear that pork can be substituted for it in all these recipes.

Roast Pork
To roast Pork without the skin

This recipe comes from Mrs Woolley's *Cook's Guide*:

> *Take any small joynt of Pork, and lay it to roast till it will pill [peel]; then pill it and stick it with Rosemary and Cloves, then baste it with butter and salt, make sawce for it with bread, water, claret wine, beaten Cinnamon boyled together; then put in butter, vinegar and sugar.*

Mrs Woolley does not say what to do with the crackling, but I can't imagine a joint of pork *without* crackling being very popular at most tables. In adapting the recipe I've given two versions, one in which the rind is left on, and the other which follows Mrs Woolley more closely.

2½–3lb/1–1.25kg leg or fillet of pork boned and rolled	*½pt/300ml red wine*
	6 cloves
A few sprigs of rosemary	*2 teaspoons cinnamon*
2oz/50g butter	*2oz/50g breadcrumbs*
1 dessertspoon raw cane sugar	*Red wine vinegar*

Preheat the oven to Gas Mark 5/190°C/375°F.

Brush the rind of the joint with oil or fat in the usual way, season with salt and freshly ground black pepper and stick both the rind and the meat of the joint with cloves and half the rosemary. Pour half the wine and a little water into a roasting tin. Roast the prepared joint on a rack in the roasting tin, allowing 30–35 minutes per pound plus 30 minutes, basting regularly.

To make the sauce, heat the remaining wine and the butter in a small pan, then add the breadcrumbs, cinnamon and the remaining rosemary, roughly chopped. Bring to the boil, then simmer, adding sugar and vinegar to taste – the wine makes the sauce very powerful, and the sugar helps soften it, as well as adding a touch of richness. The sauce should have about the consistency of single (thin) cream; if it seems too thick, add a little water, or wine if you have a strong palate.

When the meat is ready, transfer it to a carving dish and add the juices from the roasting tin to the sauce.

If you want to follow Mrs Woolley more closely, roast the joint for 30 minutes without the cloves and rosemary, then take it out of the oven and remove the outer rind by cutting the strings and running a knife between the fat and the skin. Stick the cloves and rosemary into the uncovered meat and return to the oven. It is a slightly tricky operation, and as one wrestles with recalcitrant semi-crackling and stubborn string, gradually getting covered with congealing pork fat while doing so, one is forcibly reminded that Mrs Woolley had cook-maids to do this sort of thing for her. Such moments of realisation support my feeling that the kitchen is one of the most vivid theatres of social history in the world.

Baste the meat at regular intervals to ensure that it does not become dry. Despite the messy procedure, removing the skin (which can be baked to crackling point separately) does mean that the meat is suffused much more thoroughly with the wine and herbs when basted.

Serves 4–6.

Here is another example of Mrs Woolley's preference for steaks cut from the leg joint, rather than chops from the ribs.

Grilled Steaks of Pork with Mustard Sauce
To broyl a Leg of Pork

Once again, a simple but very effective way of preparing a fairly standard cut of meat, either pork steaks or chops. Some people prefer chops as having more flavour, because they are cooked with the bone in. Loin chops, trimmed of fat, are good for this recipe. The original is for steaks:

Cut your Pork into slices very thin . . . then hack it with the back of your Knife, then mince some Thyme and Sage exceeding small, and mingle it with Pepper and Salt, and therewith season your Collops, and then lay them on the Grid-Iron . . .

The broyling method, as used in the recipe for grilled lamb, is clearly displayed here – these would also do well on a barbeque.

4 steaks cut from a leg of pork	1oz/25g butter
1 tablespoon each of fresh thyme and sage, finely chopped	Salt and pepper

For the sauce:

2oz/50g butter	1 tablespoon good mustard, preferably wholegrain
1–2 dessertspoons raw cane sugar	2 tablespoons wine or cider vinegar

Arrange the steaks on the grill, sprinkle with the herbs and season to taste. Dab them with butter and cook under a moderate grill for 6 minutes each side. .

For the sauce, melt the butter in a small pan, then stir in the mustard, vinegar and as much sugar as you want. Bring to a foaming boil, then stir over medium heat until the sugar has dissolved into the rest of the ingredients. The sauce smells much hotter than it actually tastes, so don't be alarmed if a sniff of it makes your eyes water. (People have varying opinions about the proportions of the different ingredients, but the sauce is so easy to make that, to save them the embarrassment of arguing with their host, I just let them do it themselves. This is called 'altruism'.)

When the 'collops' are ready, transfer them to a serving plate and add any juice from the grill pan to the sauce, which is best served separately – apart from anything else, you can keep it hot more easily in a pre-warmed jug.

Serves 4.

In the original of the next recipe, it is not clear quite which cut of meat is to be used, merely that that it should be cut thin. Hence my anachronistic use of escalopes, which seem to fit the bill.

Escalopes of Pork or Veal with Lemon and Anchovy Sauce
Scotch Collops

What we now rather daintily call 'escalopes' used to be known, especially in northern England and Scotland, as collops, although there is no etymological connection between the two words. Perhaps the English adoption of the French term indicates a newly-acquired European sensibility, or maybe it's simply the old-fashioned gastronomic snobbery which gives us 'French fried potatoes' instead of 'chips' on restaurant menus. Mrs Woolley says these collops can be made from beef, veal or mutton, though I've found the mixture of flavours best suits veal or pork.

The sauce, like that in the previous dish, has the great advantage of being made very quickly and easily, as opposed to the flour-based sauces of classic French cuisine. Indeed, Mrs Woolley's whole approach to making sauce is rather *nouvelle* – she tends to base them on the juices from the meat (as here), and thicken them with butter or egg yolks. The original recipe, which shows Mrs Woolley using the glowing, banked-up coal to the side of the main fire, is easier to follow than some:

> *Cut your meat very thin, then beat it with a Rowling pin till it be very tender; then salt it a little, and fry it in a pan without any liquor, and when it is enough, take some butter and the gravy out of the Pan, and a little Vinegar, or the juyce of a Lemmon, and some Anchoves, set it on the coales till the Anchoves be dissolved; then put your meat into a dish, and pour the sawce over it.*

I was a little wary of frying the collops without oil or butter, but they produce a great deal of their own juice, and in a non-stick frying pan are easy to handle. If you cannot get hold of escalopes, boneless steaks of pork are a good alternative.

Four escalopes of veal or pork, *The juice of a lemon*
 6–8oz/200–225g each *8 anchovy fillets*
2oz/50g butter *Salt*

Tenderize the meat with a meat hammer, the back of a heavy knife or, like Mrs Woolley, a rolling pin. (If you are cooking steaks, pound them until they are appreciably thinner than when you started – it may take a little time, but it's wonderful for working off aggression.) Salt the escalopes lightly, and fry them over a moderate heat in a non-stick pan, or melt a knob of butter in an ordinary pan first. Cook the collops for about 4 minutes on each side.

Meanwhile, chop the anchovy fillets as finely as possible, then mash them with a fork until they are reduced to a paste.

When the escalopes are done – when no pink juice flows out when pricked with a knife – take them out of the pan and keep them warm in a serving dish. Add the butter to the pan and let it melt. Then add the mashed anchovy fillets and the lemon juice and stir well. Cook over a moderate heat for 3 or 4 minutes, then pour the sauce over the escalopes and serve immediately.

A de luxe version of this dish can be made by stirring a little single cream into the sauce just before serving.

Serves 4.

Here is another recipe along the same lines, this time for veal, but with an egg-thickened sauce which is typical of Mrs Woolley's cooking.

Escalope of Veal with Egg and Lemon Sauce
To make a Fricacie of Veal

This dish takes only a few minutes to prepare, and the egg-and-lemon sauce is especially delicious, being at once creamy and refreshingly sharp. The mixture of verjuice (see page 35) and beaten egg was a very common seventeenth-century liaison, or 'caudle', as Mrs Woolley calls it, and it's certainly simpler than making sauce with a roux. You can use pork steaks or escalopes instead of veal; it responds well to the treatment suggested by Mrs Woolley: *Cut your Veal in thin slices, beat it well with a Rowling-pin . . .*

4 veal escalopes	*Salt and pepper*
1oz/25g butter	*Verjuice made with one lemon*
Juice of a lemon	*(see page 35)*
A nutmeg	*1 large egg, beaten*
1 tablespoon fresh thyme,	
finely chopped	

Tenderize the veal with your preferred blunt instrument. Grate fresh nutmeg on to both sides of each escalope, sprinkle on the thyme and season with salt and pepper. Melt the butter in a large frying pan and put in the escalopes. Pour the lemon juice

*over them and stir, then fry over a gentle heat for 2–3 minutes
each side. (If you use pork steaks, double the cooking time.)*

*Mix the beaten egg with the prepared verjuice, and when the
meat is cooked, gradually stir it into the pan, mixing it well with
the cooking liquid. Continue cooking, stirring all the time, until
the egg is fully cooked and the sauce has achieved a creamy
consistency – it's important not to turn the heat up too high, or
the egg hardens. Serve the escalopes coated in the sauce.*

Serves 4.

Quite why these little pies were given their strange name I haven't
been able to discover – perhaps it's just a local dialect name, like
Shropshire's fidget pie, whose meaning has become obscure over the
years.

Spicy Veal Pies
Stump Pies

These are ancestors of modern mince pies. They used to be a mixture
of chopped or minced meat, dried fruit and spices, sometimes with
the addition of suet. Gradually the proportion of meat declined,
until it vanished altogether, leaving as a reminder only the name and
the suet. The original of stump pie contains more than twice as much
fruit as veal; I've redressed the balance a little, but do feel free to
experiment with the proportions, and with the spices – Mrs Woolley
simply says 'ground spice', leaving the choice to the cook.

As it stands, the recipe might make a good alternative for those
who find the usual mince pies too sweet – as, indeed, might the lamb
pie recipe given on page 52. As with the lamb pies, you can make
these with hot-water crust, or with ordinary shortcrust, like mince
pies. In the latter case, make eight small pies rather than four larger
ones. These can be made with pork – the best bet is probably
shoulder, which can be bought ready cubed from most butchers,
and chopped up a bit more at home.

For the pastry:
12oz/340g wholemeal flour
4oz/100g lard or vegetable fat
10oz/300g chopped pie veal
1oz/25g currants
2oz/50g raisins
2oz/50g dried dates
7fl oz/200ml milk

For the filling:
1 teaspoon salt
2 teaspoons each ground
    cinnamon and ginger
3 teaspoons grated nutmeg
2 egg yolks, beaten
2 teaspoons rosewater

Preheat the oven to Gas Mark 7/220°C/425°F.

Mix together the veal, fruit and spices – the easiest way is to put them all into a blender for a few seconds. The veal should not be too finely minced. Turn the mixture out into a bowl and stir in the rosewater and about half the egg yolks. Season to taste.

Make the pastry following the procedure in the recipe for Lamb Pies (page 52), and fill the pies. Brush the tops with the remaining egg yolk, make a small hole in the top of each pie, and bake on a greased baking sheet in a hot oven (Gas Mark 7/ 220°C/425°F) for 10 minutes. Lower the heat to Gas Mark 5/ 190°C/375°F and bake for about another 30 minutes, until the tops are nicely golden brown.

Serves 4–6.

SAUSAGES

The sausage is one of the most emotive of all foods. In his thirties novel *Coming Up for Air*, George Orwell uses a disgusting, fish-filled, rubber-skinned sausage for symbolic purposes: 'It gave me the feeling that I'd bitten into the modern world and discovered what it was really made of.'

People have strong feelings about this apparently humble food, and will often go to great lengths to find the 'perfect' sausage. The modern article is, by and large, not a very pleasant object, at least in Britain, and it is not surprising that 'Where are the sausages of yesteryear?' is a common cry. A friend remembers with great affection the butcher's handmade special sausages she ate as a child, and my father spent years trying to find sausages as good as those he ate before the war. *His* father, in turn, recalled the 'proper' sausages from his youth before the Great War – a period in which the critic and oenologist George Saintsbury was already bemoaning the passing of the fine sausages of Victorian England. I do not have the space to follow this eternal disillusionment all the way back to Mrs Woolley's time, but her recipes for making and cooking sausages are an excellent antidote to Orwell's 'bombs of filth bursting in your mouth' – a pretty fair description of some of the alleged sausages on offer today.

Fried Sausages
To make good Sausages

Mrs Woolley's sausages are skinless, which makes them fairly easy to prepare. They are best made with lean, minced pork, as commercial sausagemeat, however good, tends to have a high proportion of fat and nearly always contains preservatives. Mrs Woolley would not have seen the need for them, as her recipe shows:

> *Take some Pork, not too fat, mince it fine, then stamp it in a Morter; season it with Pepper, Salt, Nutmegs, and a little Sage; then beat it well together, and when it is enough, keep it in Gallypots as long as you please . . .*

(Gallypots were earthenware jars used for storing ointments and various foodstuffs.) In the original, the sausages are dipped in beaten egg yolk before frying, which I find a little too rich, but you may like to try it.

1lb/450g pork sausagemeat or minced pork	*Butter for frying*
	Fresh nutmeg
A good handful of fresh sage, chopped	*Salt and pepper*
	2 beaten egg yolks (optional)

Put the pork and sage into a bowl and grate on as much nutmeg as you fancy (a minimum of half a nut). Season to taste and mix together thoroughly, then press it hard together into a ball.

Divide the mixture into four and roll it out on a well-floured board by hand (Mrs Woolley's instruction is to 'roul them in your hand like a Sausage', which is straightforward enough.) Subdivide as you roll them, until you end up with the size and number you prefer – it's a good idea to make them quite small, as they are easier to cook.

If you are using the egg yolk, spread them on a plate and roll the sausages in them. Next, melt some butter in a frying pan and fry the sausages gently for 10–12 minutes, turning them regularly to ensure that they are cooked right through.

Serves 4.

Spiced Sausages with Red Wine Sauce
To boile sawsages

Mrs Woolley's recipe for boiled 'sawsages' is her shortest:

> *Boile them in claret wine, large mace, and sweet herbs.*

About their composition, though, she is silent, so I have taken some hints from her recipe for Polonia sausages, which were put into skins and smoked hanging in the chimney above the fire. Thus preserved, they kept for months.

For the sausages:

1lb/450g sausagemeat or minced pork	1 teaspoon ground ginger
1 teaspoon ground nutmeg	½ teaspoon ground cloves
½ teaspoon ground coriander	½ teaspoon aniseed
	Salt and pepper

For the sauce:

½pt/300ml red wine	1 teaspoon ground mace
1 tablespoon chopped fresh herbs – parsley, rosemary, thyme, tarragon, etc.	Butter for frying

Mix together the sausagemeat and spices, season well and roll out the sausages as described in the previous recipe.

To cook them, first fry gently in a little butter: this ensures that they do not break up in the wine. Add the chopped herbs and mace, stir well and cook for one minute. Pour the wine over the sausages, bring to the boil briefly, then lower the heat to medium and cook for about 10 minutes, turning regularly. There should be enough wine to almost cover the sausages, but not too much; it will gradually reduce in cooking to form a rich sauce, which can be poured over the sausages when served.

These are best accompanied by mashed potatoes, which form a perfect vehicle for the sauce. However, Mrs Woolley suggests other ways to enjoy them:

> *These Sausages wil keep for a whole Year; and are good for Sallets, or to garnish boyled Meats, or to relish a Glass of Wine.*

I can easily imagine someone like Pepys 'relishing' his claret with a Polonia sausage. This, by the way, is one of my personal favourites among all Mrs Woolley's recipes.

Serves 4.

RABBIT

Rabbits were brought to Britain from France in the twelfth century. They were bred for both their food and their skins, and were much too expensive for most people – almost exclusively the preserve of the rich. It was only when the strictly guarded warrens started to fall into disuse, and rabbits became established in the wild that their numbers increased enough for them to become the cheap food of ordinary country people. Their popularity as well as their numbers declined again with the deliberate introduction of myxomatosis, which led to the import of frozen Chinese rabbits, but with the waning of the disease, fresh animals are available once more. Mrs Woolley's recipes treat them with the respect due to a delicacy.

Rabbit with Grapes, or Gooseberries
To boil a Rabbit with Grapes or Gooseberries

I have telescoped the two sections of Mrs Woolley's original recipe, which starts:

> *Truss your Rabbit whole, and boil it in some Mutton Broth till it be tender . . .*

and goes on to give the ingredients for a 'broth' or sauce to be made separately. I found that the flavour was much improved if the rabbit was cooked in the broth or sauce, and of course it makes the cooking process simpler. To serve four or five people, a rabbit weighing about 2–2½ pounds (1kg) should be ample. If you use gooseberries rather than grapes, it's worth scalding them first, with a little sugar.

1 rabbit, skinned and trussed	1 tablespoon each of fresh
1oz/25g butter	thyme, parsley and sage,
½pt/300ml good beef stock	chopped
½pt/300ml white wine	6oz/175g white grapes or
3 blades of mace	gooseberries
Salt and pepper	2 hard-boiled egg yolks
A good handful of spinach,	Wholemeal toast (optional)
chopped	

Melt the butter in a saucepan and add the rabbit. Cook over a moderate heat, turning frequently, until it is browned all over.

Add the wine and simmer for a couple of minutes, then pour in the stock, add the mace and chopped spinach and herbs, season to taste and bring to the boil. Turn down the heat, cover, and cook over a gentle heat for about 45 minutes, stirring occasionally.

Add the grapes or gooseberries and cook for another 15 minutes, or until the rabbit is tender.

Take up the rabbit and transfer it to a heated serving dish. Reduce the liquid over a high heat, if necessary, until it is quite thick. Mash the egg yolks with a little of the cooking liquid. Turn down the heat, and stir in the egg yolks. Heat the sauce through, stirring constantly, pour it over the rabbit and serve.

'Sippets' – pieces of bread or toast for mopping up the juice – are the recommended accompaniments.

Serves 4–5.

Here is a recipe made with apples, which differs from the chicken with apples on page 71, in that the flavour comes from a blend of spices rather than from dried fruit.

Rabbit Stewed with Ginger and Apples
To Stew a Rabbit

The original recipe is more complicated than my adaptation:

> *Half-Roast it, then take it off the Spit, and cut it into little pieces, and put it into a Dish with the Gravy . . .*

It would have been roasted on a small spit attached to the main spit, and turned by manual or animal labour, along with whatever birds, fish or sides of beef were also being roasted. In the seventeenth-century kitchen, because of the amount of fuel and labour it took to keep the spit operating, it was worth putting a great many different things on it. However, without having to worry about such considerations, I've found that the rabbit tastes pretty good stewed, without the preliminary roasting.

A rabbit, skinned and jointed	2 teaspoons cinnamon
Butter for frying	¾pt/450ml good stock
4 teaspoons ground ginger	Pepper and salt
2 teaspoons ground coriander	2–3 eating apples, cored and grated

Melt the butter in a saucepan and fry the rabbit pieces until well browned. Sprinkle on the ground spices, stir and fry for another minute, then add enough of the stock to cover the meat. Season to taste and bring to the boil. Then turn down the heat to a simmer, cover and cook for about an hour, or until the meat is very tender (it may take longer).

After 30 minutes, add the grated apple. At the end of the cooking time the sauce should be quite thick, like single cream.

Serve with croûtons of wholemeal toast, and/or mashed potatoes.

Serve 4–5.

VENISON

Venison has long been a preserve of the rich which is a pity, because as well as being absolutely delicious, it is a very healthy meat, having very little fat compared to beef. It's certainly worth trying on a special occasion, and if you don't finish the whole saddle in one sitting, here's a recipe to help finish it up.

Rechauffé of Venison
To Stew Venison

This uses leftover venison to make a quick supper dish. The original gives a vivid glimpse of seventeenth-century domestic economy in a large household:

> *If you have much Venison, and do make many cold baked Meats, you may stew a Dish in hast thus: When it is sliced out of your Pye, Pot, or Pasty, put it in your stewing-Dish, and set it on a heap of coals . . .*

This passage always conjures up for me a scene of frenzied activity in the kitchen, as the cook rifles the contents of great ruined pies and half-finished pasties to recycle them as a stew, perhaps for unexpected guests. As few of us are in the happy position of having 'much Venison', I'm glad to say that it works almost as well with cold beef or lamb.

1lb/450g cooked venison or
   other meat, cut in 1in/2cm
   squares
2fl oz/60ml red wine vinegar
6fl oz/175ml red wine
4 cloves

1 dessertspoon muscovado
   sugar
2 sprigs rosemary
½ nutmeg
2–3 tablespoons fine
   wholemeal breadcrumbs

Put all the ingredients except the meat into a saucepan and bring almost to the boil, then turn the heat down and add the meat. Grate on the nutmeg, cover and simmer for about 30 minutes. Adjust the seasoning before serving.
   Serves 4.

POULTRY

NOWADAYS the English eat a far smaller range of poultry and game birds than they used to, though this is due more to legislation against killing them than any particular gastronomic fastidiousness. Huge numbers of small birds were trapped with lime spread on trees, and netted, as well as being shot in large quantities – as they still are in modern Italy, where every spring the air resounds with gunfire that has nothing to do with the Mafia. As a result a town like Assisi, which through St Francis has close associations with birdlife, is, ironically, sadly lacking in birdsong. It is to Britain's credit that we can no longer order a basket of plover's eggs for a lunch party, like Sebastian Flyte, and it would be illegal, as well as possibly rather unpleasant, to eat the Elizabethan 'Tart to Provoke Courage in a Man or Woman', which involves half a dozen larks' brains.

The most famous songbird recipe from Mrs Woolley's century is, of course, the one celebrated in the nursery rhyme. However, the four-and-twenty blackbirds were not really baked in the pie, just temporarily imprisoned, to be released as part of a spectacular dinner-party warm-up. They formed the climax to a sequence of lavish 'Triumphs', or elaborate confections in pastry, much in vogue in the first half of the seventeenth century, especially 'at Festival Times, as Twelfth Day, &c.' – Twelfth Night being a bigger celebration than Christmas Day itself at this period. In Robert May's *The Accomplisht Cook*, published in 1661 but recalling an already vanished era, full details are given: a finely detailed pastry battleship exchanges fire with a miniature castle; a pastry stag, filled with claret, bleeds most realistically when punctured by an arrow, and, at the climax, the host invites the guests, all unsuspecting, to open two great pies. Out jump live frogs, which frighten the ladies, and some blackbirds, which naturally fly at the candles and put them out by flapping their wings. Confusion and panic reign; but then servants come in with more lights, music and a banquet, 'and everyone with much delight and content rehearses their actions in the former passages'.

This sort of extravagance had mostly vanished with the Civil War, though, and Mrs Woolley would have none of it. She would perhaps have been more in sympathy with another remarkable woman of the seventeenth century, Celia Fiennes, who between 1685 and 1710 visited every county in England on horseback – quite an achievement, considering the state of the roads, especially for a woman of that period. She was in Chesterfield in 1697, and noted the existence of a North/South divide when it came to poultry:

> I bought myself 2 very good full white pullets for 6 pence both, and I am sure they . . . would have cost 18 pence if not 2 shillings apiece in London.

More practical, and certainly less nostalgic than May, Mrs Woolley gives recipes that are to be eaten for birds which we still eat today: pigeons, pheasants, chickens and capons. Many of the chicken recipes in this chapter are adapted from recipes for capon, the castrated cock specially fattened for the table. Capons can be hard to come by, though they are becoming more common. If your butcher can find you one, you will need to increase quantities, as they are a good deal larger than the average chicken.

Generally speaking, poultry at this period would have been tougher, but perhaps more flavoursome than the battery-reared hens of today, hence the frequency with which it was boiled rather than roasted. If you don't like boiled meat, try roasting the chicken in the usual way and serving the sauce separately. (If you can find a butcher who sells free-range chickens, do try them for they have a much better flavour.)

I've selected a number of variations on chicken casserole, though that hardly covers the variety of ways in which Mrs Woolley can 'boil' a chicken, and two recipes for pigeon.

Chicken Stewed with Fruit and Herbs
To boil a Capon after the French fashion

Thinking up a suitable title for this dish was quite difficult, as it contains so many different things. Perhaps the rich mixture of herbs, spices, dates, currants and ground almonds was peculiarly French, though the recipe bears little similarity to the beef 'in the French

Fashion' on page 39, and just a passing resemblance to the 'Dutch' pigeons on page 77. In Mrs Woolley's original, the capon is boiled 'in water and salt, and a little dusty Oatmeal to make it look white', and the sauce is poured over it just before serving. As in other versions of her recipes, I've adapted this, and cooked the chicken in the broth. If you want to roast your chicken, simply make the sauce separately, following the instructions in the recipe.

3½lb/1½kg chicken	*Salt and pepper*
¾pt/450ml good beef stock	*3–4 blades of mace*
6 dates, sliced	*About ½ nutmeg, grated*
A good handful of mixed fresh	*Verjuice made with one lemon*
* thyme, parsley and*	*2 dessertspoons ground*
* rosemary, chopped*	* almonds*
2oz/50g currants	*2oz/50g butter*
	2 teaspoons sugar (or to taste)

Put the chicken into a saucepan, pour in the stock and add enough water to just cover the bird. Put in the dates, herbs, currants, mace and nutmeg, season to taste and bring to the boil. Cover and simmer gently for about an hour, which should be enough for the standard roasting chicken.

Take out the chicken when it is tender, transfer it to a deep serving dish and keep it warm. Boil the broth rapidly to reduce it a little, then lower the heat slightly and add the verjuice. Stir in the almonds and the butter and as much of the sugar as you like. Cook for a few more minutes over a moderate heat, then pour the sauce over the chicken and serve. The sauce should be quite thin – don't be tempted into adding more ground almond to thicken it, as this spoils the balance of the flavours.

Have lots of wholemeal bread available for mopping up the delicious sauce. If you are cooking the dish with chicken pieces, reduce cooking time to about 15–20 minutes, or until tender.

Serves 4–6.

The variety of ways in which Mrs Woolley treated poultry is exemplified in the difference between that rich and sweet dish and this one, in which fresh, as opposed to dried, fruit, is the predominating flavour, giving it a delicious and unusual tang.

Chicken Stewed with Oysters and Orange
To make a fricasse of Chickens

This stew of chicken, which at first glance might seem fairly unusual, actually has many international parallels to its mixture of meat with oysters: America has carpetbagger steak, the Portuguese cook pork with oysters, and oysters were a standard ingredient in the original Lancashire hotpot. The presence of oysters in the latter dish, and the copious way in which Mrs Woolley uses them in many of her recipes, is a reminder that in her day they were a cheap and common food. Robert May used their juice to flavour dishes as a modern cook might use Worcester sauce. Nowadays they arrive at the diner's table as a distinct status symbol, which is rather a pity, and dishes which include them do so to emphasise the wealth of the consumer, rather than the cheapness of the oyster.

If you are not actually that keen on oysters, or they are not available, the dish is still very good without them. You can use mussels, which are cheaper, instead; take them out of the shells before cooking and continue as before, except for slightly increasing the quantity. Or you can use tinned oysters, which although generally smaller and saltier than the fresh variety – and some people don't like their tinned flavour – are useful as a last resort when no fresh shellfish is available.

1½lb/675g boned chicken, cut in small pieces	2 teaspoons fresh grated nutmeg
½–¾pt/450ml white wine	Grated peel and juice of an orange
1 tablespoon each of fresh parsley, thyme and rosemary, or 2 teaspoons each dried	6 oysters
	1 egg, beaten
	1–2oz/25–50g butter

Put the chicken, herbs, nutmeg and orange peel into a deep frying pan and pour over enough of the wine to cover. Bring to the boil, then lower the heat, half cover and simmer for about 20 minutes, or until the chicken pieces are white and tender.

Then add the oysters, with some of the juice from their shells if using fresh oysters, and the orange juice. Continue cooking for another 2 or 3 minutes, until the oysters are done – be careful not to overcook them, because they go rather tough. With a slotted spoon transfer the chicken and shellfish to a warm serving dish.

Add 1oz/25g butter to the sauce and let it melt, then remove

the pan from the heat and allow to cool for a moment. Stir a
tablespoon of the sauce into the beaten egg, then gradually stir
this mixture back into the rest of the sauce. Return to the heat
and keep stirring until the sauce has thickened to about the
consistency of single (thin) cream.

Pour over the chicken and oysters and serve with rice or
potatoes and a light salad – as the dish is quite rich, not much in
the way of accompaniment is really needed.

(For a really luxurious version, use chicken breasts, cut into
1in/2cm squares, and reduce the cooking time slightly.)

Serves 4.

That dish is unusual for Mrs Woolley, not so much because of the
oysters, but because of her instruction to 'cut your meat in little
pieces'. Generally she cooks her chickens or capons whole, and
smothers them with sauce, as in the next recipe. This traditionally
English, indeed West Country dish of chicken with apples might
well pass as that authentic French dish, *poulet Normande*, in some
contemporary restaurants – a fact which, once again, shows that
'national' cuisine, like national folk music, is not as different from
one country to the next as is often thought.

Chicken with Apples
To boile a Capon with Pippins

This can be made either with a whole chicken – a good old-fashioned
boiling fowl is very good, if you can get one – or with chicken pieces,
as here. (If you make it with a whole bird, follow the instructions for
'Chicken Stewed with Fruit and Herbs' on page 68.) The original
recipe is written in a slightly slapdash manner, and it took me a while
to work out a convenient way of making it. I quote it in full to give
some idea of the problems involved in tackling Mrs Woolley's
.instructions – this is a good example of her more obscure style:

Parboile you Capon in water and salt, then put the marrow of two or
three good bones into a pipkin with a quart of white wine, a little sliced
nutmegg, four or five dates, and some sugar; then pare some Pippins
and cut them in quarters, put them into a pipkin and cover them with
sugar and water; then make sippets of biskets, then take the yolks of

height hard eggs and strain them with a little Verjuice, and some of the broth wherein the capon is boiled, put them to the pippins with a little sack, stir them together, and so serve the capon in with them.

The problem with these instructions is that the relationship of the marrow bones, wine and dates with the rest of the dish is never explained. In adapting it, I have (as usual) cooked the chicken in the wine, with stock replacing the bone-marrow (but if you can get it, do use it, as it adds a very individual flavour and texture to the sauce). I've also increased the quantity of dates, and reduced the number of egg yolks, though this is a purely personal preference. This recipe makes quite a lot of sauce, which is a good thing – I usually find that, with any worthwhile sauce, people always ask for more, however much you make.

4 chicken pieces
½pt/300ml good stock
½pt/300ml white wine
8–10 dried dates, sliced
  lengthways
1 teaspoon sugar
1 nutmeg, grated
Salt to taste

12oz/340g eating apples,
  peeled, cored and chopped
3 hard-boiled egg yolks
Verjuice made with one lemon
1 tablespoon medium sweet
  sherry (optional)

Put the chicken, stock, wine, dates and sugar into a saucepan and grate on the nutmeg. Season lightly and bring to the boil, then cover and simmer for about 20 minutes.

In a separate pan, heat the apples with a little water until they are fairly mushy; this should take about 8–10 minutes.

Mash the egg yolks with the verjuice and sherry until they form a paste, then mix it all thoroughly into the apple purée. Stir well over a low heat.

Take the chicken pieces from the saucepan and keep them warm in a serving dish. Stir enough of the cooking liquid into the apple mixture to produce a fairly runny sauce – the exact amount depends, of course, on how you like your sauce. Add as many of the sliced dates as possible – they give the dish its distinctive flavour.

Adjust the seasoning, pour some of the sauce over the chicken, and serve the rest in a warmed sauceboat. (This is also good with pigeon.)

Serves 4.

The unusual name of the next dish, like that of 'Smoored Lamb' (page 48) refers to a seventeenth-century cook-in sauce – the word 'smoor' being an old word meaning to smother – in this case, with a sharp and refreshing lemony sauce.

Chicken Pieces Fried with Verjuice
To Smoor Chickens

This is slightly unusual among Mrs Woolley's poultry recipes in that the chicken is fried first, then cooked in a sauce of wine, herbs and verjuice, rather than just being boiled. The original recipe posed one problem, though:

> . . . *fry the Leaves of Clary with Eggs, put a little Salt to your Chickens, and when they are enough, serve them in this fryed Clary.*

My complete failure to track down clary, an aromatic plant of the same family as sage, led me to consider this particular dish a non-starter, but I found that the combination of apple verjuice, herbs and wine was delicious even without the elusive herb. (I've used a little sage instead, which, while not absolutely authentic, tastes good.)

As for the garnish, Mrs Woolley uses barberries, orange or red berries often used in the making of medicinal tonics. These are hard to come by in the shops (and in most people's gardens), so I have suggested cranberries. The substitution was first practised by early settlers in America, who couldn't find barberries – hence the traditional roast turkey with cranberry sauce at Thanksgiving. The colour combination of fresh green parsley and deep red berries is highly attractive.

4 chicken joints	Butter for frying
2 medium onions, finely chopped	A good handful of fresh parsley, chopped
½pt/300ml white wine	1 dessertspoon fresh chopped sage or 1 teaspoon dried
Verjuice made with two lemons	2 blades of mace
Salt and pepper	2 egg yolks (optional)
Cranberries to garnish	

Melt the butter in a deepish frying pan and fry the chicken pieces until they are lightly coloured. Add the onions, continue frying gently for 5 minutes until they are soft, then add the liquid, herbs and mace. Season to taste and bring to the boil, then lower the heat and simmer, half covered, for 20–30 minutes.

When tender, take the chicken pieces out of the pan and keep hot on a serving dish, then add a little of the sauce to the beaten yolks, mix well and stir this liaison back into the remaining liquid. Pour the sauce over the chicken, garnish with the berries and serve.

Serves 4.

These dishes – mighty capons, dripping with rich sauce, brought to table in great profusion – would have been main dishes for either the first or second course at dinner, taking their place with the roasts. This salad would probably have been one of the table-fillers, a smaller titbit among the heavy artillery. There might easily have been sixteen main dishes and the same number of side dishes at a substantial middle-class dinner, and many more at a meal for the nobility, so it's hardly surprising that little was eaten in the evenings.

Chicken Salad
A Sallet of a Cold Hen or Pullet

Mrs Woolley, like other cooks, borrowed from a collection called *The Court and Kitchen of Elizabeth commonly called Joan Cromwell*, published in 1664. This purported to be by Oliver Cromwell's widow, though as only a couple of recipes in it have a personal connection, it seems probable that issuing it under her name was a publisher's gimmick. This 'Sallet' first appeared there and obviously struck Mrs Woolley as a good thing, which indeed it is, being ideal for using up leftover roast chicken. She recommends garnishing the dish with the peel of the lemon and the bones of the chicken, but I'm afraid this doesn't appeal to me very much, and I just use lemon peel.

8oz/225g cooked chicken, chopped
A small onion, peeled and chopped
Two eating apples, cored and chopped

A lemon, peeled and chopped
2 tablespoons chopped fresh parsley
Salt and pepper to taste
Oil and vinegar

Mix all the ingredients together except for the oil and vinegar; make a dressing from these and lightly toss the salad in it just before serving. If you like, peel the lemon in long strips and use these to decorate the salad plate.

Serves 4 as a side salad, or 2 as a main dish.

As its original title shows, the next recipe was for a dish designed to use up the innards of rabbits which had presumably been roasted or stewed. However, as chicken livers are much easier to get hold of these days than rabbits', I decided to make it with the former, and interpolate the recipe in this chapter.

Chicken Liver Pasties
A made Dish of Rabbits Livers

These pasties were described by Mrs Woolley as a 'made Dish' because they were not roasted or boiled meat, but 'baked meats', like the ones which 'coldly furnished forth the marriage table' in *Hamlet*. Their ingredients show Mrs Woolley indulging once again in the seventeenth-century habit of mixing dried fruit with meat. Like the apple pasties on page 115 they can be either baked or fried.

8oz/225g chicken livers	*1oz/25g butter*
1 tablespoon chopped fresh herbs: parsley, thyme, rosemary, etc	*Yolks of 2 hard-boiled eggs*
	1 teaspoon crushed allspice
	2oz/50g currants
For the pastry:	
8oz/225g flour	*4oz/100g butter*
Pinch of salt	*Water*

Chop the livers and egg yolks and mix together with the herbs, currants and spice; season to taste and fry gently in the butter for 5 or 6 minutes. Leave to cool.

Make up the pastry and roll it out very thin, then cut 8–10 circles from it. Put a little of the mixture on to one half of each circle, brush the edges with milk, fold over and seal.

Fry the pasties in extra butter for about 4–5 minutes on each side, making sure the butter really coats the pastry and that the

pasties are browned all over. Serve hot. Alternatively, bake them, in which case the mixture need not be cooked before-hand; however, in this case a flaky or puff pastry is better than an ordinary shortcrust.
    Serves 4.

PIGEON

Judging by Mrs Woolley's recipes, it is possible to deduce that, in one respect at least, things have not changed in the last 300 years: pigeons were, and are, much better casseroled than roasted. Their unpopularity in some quarters may be due to unfortunate experiences attempting to eat the dry, tough, roast variety, when in fact their unique and powerful flavour is ideally suited to long cooking in a tasty sauce. The two recipes I have adapted show that Mrs Woolley recognised that pigeon makes a good vehicle for strong sauces, as its own flavour is robust enough to stand up to them.

Pigeons with Grapes
To boil Chickens or Pideons with Gooseberries, or Grapes

A favourite way of cooking poultry or rabbits was with grapes or gooseberries, depending on what was in season, and the length of your purse. The title of this recipe gives the cook several options; I decided on pigeons and grapes, because they go so well together. It is also a practical combination, because they're both available all the year round, and the cheapness of the poultry makes up for the expense of the fruit. The colour of the grapes here is really a matter of aesthetics; Mrs Woolley doesn't specify one or the other, but presumably, if they are substituting for gooseberries, white grapes would be best.

4 pigeons	*4oz/100g red or white grapes*
A good handful each of fresh	*2oz/50g finely grated brown*
thyme, marjoram,	*breadcrumbs*
rosemary and savory, or	*3 hard-boiled egg yolks,*
2 teaspoons each, dried	*chopped*
½ bottle white wine	*4oz/100g butter*
8fl oz/300ml good stock	*Verjuice made with 2*
Salt and pepper	*lemons*
4 blades of mace	

Chop the herbs roughly, mix them well together and stuff each bird with some of the mixture and a blade of mace. (If you cannot get all the herbs fresh, use teaspoonfuls of dried herbs mixed to a paste with some of the butter; spread this inside the bird instead.) Put the pigeons in a deep saucepan, and pour on to them enough wine and stock to just cover them. Bring to the boil, then reduce the heat to a simmer, season to taste and cook, covered, for about 40 minutes. Put the grapes in and keep cooking for a further 20 minutes.

Take the pigeons out when they are tender, put them into a serving dish – Mrs Woolley recommends a 'boiled meat-dish' – and keep them hot.

To make the sauce, melt the butter in a saucepan, and add some of the broth from the pigeons and the verjuice. Stir well. Mash the egg yolks to a smooth paste, then mix in some of the broth and verjuice.

Add the breadcrumbs, stir well, then return it all to the main saucepan and simmer, stirring gently, for a few minutes. The sauce should have the consistency of single (thin) cream, so you may need to add more of the cooking broth.

Pour some of the sauce round the pigeons, along with the grapes, and serve the rest separately in a jug or gravy boat.

Serves 4.

Pigeon Stewed with Dried Fruit
To boyl Pigeons, the Dutch way

As with the French capon, I'm unsure about Mrs Woolley's reasons for the national title of this dish. It makes an interesting variation on the recipe for pigeon with grapes given above, and has some similarities with the French capon – which perhaps casts doubt on Mrs Woolley's accuracy of nomenclature. The original recipe shows how far we have come (downhill) in the matter of stock: where I feel virtuous in specifying a good, home-made stock, Mrs Woolley sets a rather higher standard:

> *Lard, and set your Pigeons, put them into a Pipkin, with some strong broth made of Knuckles of Veal, Mutton and Beef . . .*

Another aspect of these instructions that might strike the modern reader as unusual is the larding of poultry which is to be stewed, rather than roasted. Personally, I find the addition of extra fat, either smeared on or 'interlarded' – that is, threaded through the skin – rather unpleasant and superfluous in a casserole. However, a good result can be obtained by threading a rasher of streaky bacon over the breast and under the legs of each bird, or simply by putting a rolled-up rasher inside each one. This adds to the flavour of the finished dish, without making it much fattier.

4 pigeons
4 rashers of streaky bacon
1pt/600ml home-made beef
    stock
1 tablespoon fresh parsley,
    chopped
2 sprigs thyme and rosemary
2 blades of mace
2 tablespoons raisins
2 tablespoons capers

8 dates, roughly chopped
Salt and pepper
4oz/100g cranberries
4oz/100g butter
2oz/50g fine wholemeal
    breadcrumbs
2 egg yolks, beaten
Verjuice made with one lemon
1 teaspoon freshly grated
    nutmeg

Roll up the rashers of bacon and insert one inside each pigeon. Put the birds into a saucepan large enough for them all to sit on the bottom. Pour over the stock – it ought to almost cover them – and add the herbs, mace, raisins, capers and dates. Bring slowly to the boil, then season to taste, cover and simmer for about an hour. After 40 minutes, add the cranberries and half of the butter.

Melt the rest of the butter in a small saucepan, then take it off the heat and stir in the breadcrumbs, egg yolks and the verjuice, in that order.

When the pigeons are cooked, pour a ladleful of the cooking broth into the breadcrumb liaison and mix thoroughly. Gradually stir this mixture back into the cooking liquid – you should end up with a rich, but fairly runny sauce. Adjust the seasoning, if neccessary, add the nutmeg and transfer the whole lot to a warmed casserole for serving.

Or, if you have a cast-iron casserole of the Le Creuset type, which can be used on top of the stove, cook it and serve it in that. The pigeons should be produced from a steaming vat, exuding fascinating and irresistible perfumes, to the wonder of the waiting diners.

Serves 4.

FISH

THE number of fish recipes in Mrs Woolley's books is small compared with recipes for meat or puddings, which reflects the comparative rarity of fresh fish in the English diet of the period. Generally speaking, unless you lived near the sea in the seventeenth century, most of the fish you ate would be salted or pickled. A household would commonly have a barrel of pickled herrings for use throughout the year, and the frequent references to anchovy used as a flavouring show that salted anchovies were also popular.

Of course, people who lived near rivers were the exception: they had access to freshwater fish, and compared to the modern fishmonger's selection, they ate a very wide range of fish. Isaak Walton's *Compleat Angler*, one of the most popular books of the period, gives not only directions for catching fish but various recipes for them as well: minnow-tansies, roast eel, poached carp, pike stuffed with oysters and anchovies, broiled chub, and even gudgeon:

> The gudgeon is reputed a fish of excellent taste, and to be very wholesome . . . He is commended for a fish of excellent nourishment.

But perhaps his most attractive idea is for minnow-tansies: minnows fried with egg yolks, cowslips and primroses. I was disappointed that Mrs Woolley did not have a recipe for them.

Mrs Woolley sticks to saltwater fish, usually of the commoner kinds, and a few freshwater fish such as trout and salmon, which is probably a more accurate reflection of what was generally available to her readers. However, she has recipes for oysters: they were popular because they could be brought up to London alive, in tanks. She may also have had a particular affection for them as Essex, where she was brought up, produced the best oysters. The contemporary historian Thomas Fuller says that Colchester oysters were 'fat, salt, and green-finned'. Other popular shellfish were crayfish, which live in freshwater and could thus be eaten fresh inland, and crabs. Celia Fiennes saw 'crawfish' on sale for '2 pence a dozen' at Ripon Market, and crabs six for threepence at Knaresborough in 1697. On the whole, though, the larger shellfish were simply boiled, and I haven't found any elaborate recipies for crabs and lobsters in Mrs Woolley's books. To start this selection, I've chosen one of my favourites among all Mrs Woolley's recipes. My learned fishmonger pointed out to me that at this period 'mullet' would have meant locally-caught grey mullet, as the red mullet, which thrives in warmer waters, was not known here until much later. However, the flavour of the smaller red mullet goes so well with the rich sauce that I decided to risk the anachronism.

Red Mullet with Ginger and Garlic
Mullets Fried

Mrs Woolley's title makes this sound rather a simple dish, but it is more elaborate than the name suggests. After frying,

> *put to them some Claret-wine, sliced Ginger, grated Nutmeg, an Anchovee, Salt, and sweet Butter beaten up thick, but first rub the dish with a Clove of Garlick.*

Note the use of *sweet* butter – this would be either fresh, unsalted butter, or older butter which had kept well. (Mrs Woolley mentions elsewhere that the best time for salting down butter is in May, when the air was 'most temperate'.) Equally interesting is the use of garlic – this recipe is one of comparatively few in which Mrs Woolley uses it. Isaak Walton uses garlic in a similar way, suggesting, in a recipe for pike, that the serving dish be rubbed round with a clove of garlic 'to give the sauce a *haut-gout*'. Rubbing the frying pan here has the same effect. Try to find the juiciest pink-tinted cloves, not the small, wizened ones so often on sale in supermarkets. Mrs Woolley's advice to 'chuse the least Mullets to fry' is very sound; the smaller ones have a sweeter taste and it is easier to cook them thoroughly.

4 small red mullet	*5 fl oz / 150 ml red wine*
Butter for frying	*2 cloves of garlic, peeled*
2 oz / 50 g flour	*Nutmeg for grating*
1/2 in / 1 cm cube of fresh ginger	*2 anchovy fillets*

Scale the fish, gut them, and cut off the heads. Remove the backbones, by pressing the fish out flat with the heel of the hand and pressing down the backbone with your thumb. Then turn the fish over, loosen the ribs with a sharp knife, and prise out the bone. Lightly dust the fish with seasoned flour.

Cut the cloves of garlic in half and rub the frying pan with the cut surface (or crush the garlic and fry it in the butter). Melt some butter in the pan and fry the fish gently for 2–3 minutes each side.

Next add the wine and the anchovies, finely chopped, then grate on the ginger and as much nutmeg as pleases you. Continue cooking until the sauce has reduced almost to a glaze, adding a little more butter for richness, if desired.

Serves 4.

This next recipe for mullet, like the first, has a deceptively simple and hardly very attractive name (anything 'boiled' always sounds a little dull) but is in fact very tasty.

Poached Mullet with Claret Sauce
To boyl a Mullet

When I was trying out this recipe for the first time, I thought it was fairly easy, except for the mention of 'Butter drawn with Claret'. I only found out what it was when I discovered Mrs Woolley's instructions 'To draw Butter for Sauce': butter is melted, then water, vinegar or wine is beaten in – 'If it keep its colour white, it is good; but if yellow and turn'd, it is not to be used.' This formed the basis of many sauces, and indeed was often used on its own.

4 small mullet
¾pt/450ml water
Handful of fresh parsley,
   marjoram and thyme, or 2
   teaspoons each dried

1 dessertspoon red wine
   vinegar
2 onions, sliced
1 lemon, sliced

For the sauce:
3oz/75g butter
5fl oz/150ml claret
2 anchovy fillets, finely
   chopped

1 teaspoon freshly grated
   nutmeg
½ teaspoon ground mace
Salt and pepper

Wash, scale and gut the mullet as described in the previous recipe, but don't bone them, as they tend to fall apart in cooking.

Heat the water with the herbs, vinegar, onions and lemon, adding a little salt. When the water boils, put in the fish, lower the heat and simmer for about 8 minutes, or until the fish is tender. (There should be enough water to slightly more than cover the fish.)

Meanwhile, make the sauce by melting the butter in a small pan, then gradually stirring in the wine. Add the remaining ingredients and stir over a gentle heat for 5 minutes. The sauce should coagulate, but will not become very thick – it should be fairly runny. Season to taste (it may not need much salt because of the anchovies).

When the fish are ready, take them from the pan and drain them very thoroughly. Arrange them on a warmed serving dish, pour on the sauce and serve. Mrs Woolley suggests garnishing the dish with 'fried Oysters and Bay-leaves'. I think that bayleaves, especially fresh from the tree, make a very colourful and attractive garnish, but fried oysters are a little too rich to accompany the mullet. However, if you want to try the combination, there's a recipe for fried oysters on page 86.

Serves 4.

While mullet is quite a fashionable fish these days, plaice has the reputation of being a bit dull, suitable only for smothering in white sauce or deep-frying with chips. Mrs Woolley obviously thought differently, for she includes several recipes for it, many of which can also be used for its relative, the flounder, a fish which is held in even lower esteem these days. I've chosen two of them.

Plaice Poached in Wine and Spices
To boyle Place or Flounders

Like the ingredients in most of Mrs Woolley's recipes to 'boyle' food, the fish is not really boiled. In fact, when I first read this recipe, I was reminded of a high-class bouillion:

*Boyle them in White Wine, water and Salt, with some Cloves, Mace,
Lemmon pill, and some small Onions.*

I think that this is a preliminary cooking procedure, one of the
standard 'liquors' for poaching fish, and that the fish would be
served with a separate sauce, as it is with tartare sauce nowadays.
You could serve it simply with some 'drawn butter' (see the previous
recipe) or use a 'modern' sauce of your choice, such as tartare. I've
adapted the recipe slightly by frying the fish lightly first in seasoned
flour, as this helps give it more body.

To make the bouillion:

10fl oz/300ml white wine	A pinch of ground cloves
3–4 blades of mace	2 small onions, sliced
The finely grated peel of a	Salt and pepper
lemon	

4 whole plaice, skinned	Lemon for garnishing
Seasoned flour	(optional)
Butter for frying	

*Put all the ingredients for the bouillion into a small saucepan,
cover and bring to the boil. When it boils, take the lid off and
cook briskly until the liquid has reduced by about half. Strain it
into a jug.*

*Lightly coat the plaice in seasoned flour, then melt the butter
in a frying pan and quickly fry the fish on both sides. Pour the
bouillion over them and simmer, covered, for 10–12 minutes, or
until the fish are tender. Drain them thoroughly and transfer to
a heated serving dish; serve garnished with lemon quarters, if
liked.*

Serves 4.

This next recipe is more elaborate, perhaps indicating Mrs Woolley's
high regard for the humble flounder. I've adapted it for plaice, as
flounders are rarely available these days.

Plaice Poached with Ginger and Oysters
To stew Flounders

Although I've made it with plaice, this can in fact be made with most
white fish, and is good for gingering up (quite literally) any fish with
a bland flavour, such as plaice, whiting or coley. Mrs Woolley
emphasizes the ginger flavour by telling the reader to 'Garnish it
with Limmon, and Ginger beaten in the brims of the Dish'. Whether
this 'beaten', ie ground, ginger was for decoration or use, I'm not
sure. Mrs Woolley also casually mentions 'a few minced Oysters' –
showing how common and handy an ingredient they were. If fresh
oysters are not available, use mussels instead, or failing them, tinned
oysters. The amounts I have given here make enough for a first
course; if you want to serve the fish as a main course, use whole
plaice and increase the other ingredients proportionately.

Four 4oz/100g fillets of plaice,   *8 oysters, or more according to*
   or other white fish   *size, chopped*
10fl oz/300ml white wine   *1 medium onion, quartered*
A handful of fresh parsley and   *2oz/50g butter*
   thyme, chopped   *2 egg yolks, beaten*
Salt and pepper   *2 teaspoons dried ginger*
¾in/1½cm cube of fresh   *Lemon juice*
   ginger, grated   *4 slices wholemeal bread*

*Put the wine, onion, herbs, fresh ginger and salt and pepper in a
saucepan and simmer, covered, for about 10 minutes, to give the
flavours time to infuse. Then add the fillets and cook for another
5–8 minutes, depending on the thickness of the fish.*

   *When the fillets are almost ready, add the chopped oysters
and cook for a minute or two longer, then take up the fish,
drain, and keep warm.*

   *Toast the bread while making the sauce. Take out the onion
quarters and discard, then add the butter to the pan and, when
it has melted, take the pan off the heat and stir in the egg yolks.
Return to the heat and stir for a minute or two until the sauce
has thickened, then put each fillet on a piece of toast and pour
over the sauce.*

   *Sprinkle on some lemon juice and then some ground ginger,
and serve immediately.*

   Serves 4 as a first course.

Lastly, a very simple recipe for trout, one of the few which Mrs Woolley gives. She would not have recognised the rainbow trout so common today, as it is of North American origin, and probably would have regarded it as less flavoursome than the brown trout. This recipe is rather like a *truite meunière*, except that the wine used is specified as sweet.

Trout Poached in Sweet Wine and Herbs
To stew a Trout

The original recipe is very clear, and quite straightforward, though I was immediately surprised by the idea of sprinkling sugar on freshly cooked fish. However, it is worth trying, even if only once, and not just for reasons of historical research. Even without the sugar, the combination of fresh herbs, butter and wine is delicious. The 'sweet wine' specified might perhaps have been a Rhenish wine, occasionally mentioned in Mrs Woolley's recipes, so an appropriate modern equivalent would be a medium sweet German white.

4 trout (about 10oz/300g each), washed and gutted
4oz/100g butter
A handful each of fresh thyme, parsley and savory, chopped, or 2 teaspoons each dried

4 large blades of mace
3/4pt/450ml medium-sweet white wine
1–2 hard-boiled egg yolks
1 dessertspoon golden granulated sugar (optional)
Salt and pepper

Mash together the butter and the herbs, and season well with salt and pepper. Stuff some of the mixture inside each fish, along with a blade of mace, then put the fish into a deep frying pan – Mrs Woolley recommends 'a deep pewter Dish'. Pour over the wine, cover closely and cook over a low heat for about 15 minutes. Half way through the cooking time, turn the fish over with a slice to ensure that they are evenly cooked. When they are ready, take them up and drain them, and arrange them on a warm serving dish.

Reduce the liquid in the pan a little by fast boiling. Chop the egg yolks finely and sprinkle on the fish, together with a little sugar if desired. Serve the sauce separately – it will be fairly runny, so ensure there is bread on hand to mop it up.

Serves 4.

OYSTERS

'He was a very brave man', said James I, 'who first adventured on eating of oysters'. The pioneer who, in the poet John Gay's words,

> First broke the oozy Oyster's pearly coat
> And risqu'd the living Morsel down his Throat

started a great tradition. The taste for oysters was originally widespread, and it is only comparatively recently that they have become a luxury food. It comes as something of a shock to read Sam Weller's remark that 'poverty and oysters always seem to go together'. They were just as much of a staple for the poor in Mrs Woolley's time as in Dickens's, and some of the most famous came from Wallfleet, Whitstable and above all Colchester, in her native Essex. But one did not need to live near the coast to eat them; when they came up to London, the Woolleys would have been able to buy them on the city streets. John Gay, in his poem *Trivia*, tells the visitor to London about the local fast food:

> If where *Fleet-Ditch* with muddy Current flows,
> You chance to roam; where Oyster-Tubs in Rows
> Are ranged beside the Posts; there stay thy Haste,
> And with the sav'ry Fish indulge thy Taste.

Even towards the end of the last century it was possible for a London schoolboy to lunch off a dozen oysters, with bread and butter, for fourpence, but the decline in the native oyster industry has led to higher prices and fewer (and richer) consumers. They are still well worth eating occasionally, though, and Mrs Woolley's recipes will serve to increase the sense of occasion when one does eat them.

Oysters Fried with White Wine and Anchovies
To fry Oysters

This dish, either as an alternative savoury to Angels on Horseback or as a powerful first course, is best made with the fresh variety, but it is also a very good way of exploiting canned oysters, as the anchovy in the sauce neutralises any coarseness in them. If you use canned, increase the quantities, as they're considerably smaller than the fresh ones.

As many oysters as you think you and your guests can eat – at least a dozen for four people

Beaten egg for coating
2–3 anchovy fillets
Butter for frying
2–4fl oz/60–125ml white wine

Open the oyster shells, take out the oysters and dry them on kitchen towel. Reserve the fluid (or 'liquor' as Mrs Woolley calls it) and heat it with the anchovy fillets, finely chopped. Dip the oysters in the beaten egg, heat plenty of butter in a frying pan, and fry them gently for 2 minutes.

Pour over the anchovy liquid and white wine, and let it bubble in the pan for a minute, then serve immediately.

If you use canned oysters, drain, wash and dry them thoroughly, as they are often very salty. Use white wine to make the anchovy sauce in place of the oyster liquor. This makes quite a rich dish.

Serves 4 (and upwards)

The next recipe, in contrast, is quite a delicate way to treat oysters, in a kind of gratin. It's made easier if you have some large scallop or clam shells in which to grill the oysters.

Grilled Oysters
To broil Oysters

In the original recipe, as the name suggests, the oysters were cooked over the fire:

> Take of your largest Oysters, and put them into Scollop shells, or into the biggest Oyster shells with their own Liquor and set them upon a Gridiron over Charcoals . . .

Presumably the discarded, smaller oysters would be used for making sauces, such as that for plaice on page 84. As with the grilled steaks on page 55, for modern convenience I've adapted this recipe from the gridiron to the grill. It is a very simple and tasty dish, good either as a first course or a savoury – though of course, as it has to be prepared at the last moment, it necessitates the cook leaping up from the table at what should be the pleasantest and most relaxed time of the meal.

Plenty of oysters – a dozen	*1oz/25g butter*
for four people, ideally	*2oz/50g fine wholemeal*
Salt to taste	*breadcrumbs*

Open the oysters and detach each one from its shell. If any of the shells are particulary small, transfer the oyster into the discarded top half of one of the larger ones, or into scallop shells if you have any. Arrange the oysters on a fireproof serving dish on the grill pan and cook under a hot grill for 2–3 minutes.

Remove from the heat, add a tiny dab of butter to each one, sprinkle lightly with breadcrumbs and a pinch of salt, and return to the grill for another minute, until the breadcrumbs are golden-brown. Mrs Woolley writes:

let them stand till they are very brown; and serve them to the Table in the Shells upon a Dish and Pie-plate,

but it doesn't really matter how they're served, as long as they're served immediately.

Serves 4.

VEGETABLES AND EGGS

WHEN friends heard that I was compiling a book of seventeenth-century recipes, their first response was, nearly always, to comment on the exclusively carnivorous nature of the period. A vegetarian friend assumed automatically that there was no point in his buying a copy. (I speedily disabused him, of course.) The common assumption was that the average Englishman of the seventeenth century never let greenstuffs pass his lips, preferring to sustain himself on vast amounts of meat and strong beer, with the occasional roast swan when he could get it. This attitude probably stems, at least in part, from memories of lavish feasts re-created in Hollywood extravaganzas, but it may be due also to a sort of nostalgia, as even in these enlightened times, many people, especially men, regard a meatless meal as no kind of meal at all.

It would however be wrong to think of traditional English cooking as vegetable free. One of the reasons for the assumption is the small number of recipes for cooking vegetables found in old cookery books, but this is quite probably because the writers assumed everyone would know how to cook them. (In the same way, Mrs Woolley writes of butter: 'I need not tell you how to make Butter, since there are very few in the Country who can be ignorant thereof.') There are a lot of recipes for fancier ways of treating vegetables, like the spinach tarts and sweet potato pie given here, as well as advice on more exotic vegetables, like fennel. Salads, too, were very important, as they often formed the centrepiece of the dining table. Robert May even has a section in his *Accomplish't Cook* of purely decorative salads, as well as those for eating. In winter they relied on dried or pickled fruit and vegetables, but in friendlier seasons cooks could really go to town; Mrs Woolley begins her recipe for a 'grand Sallet' with a phrase which encapsulates how much we have lost since her day: 'Take in the spring-time, the buds of all kind of sweet herbs ...' This particular recipe is no longer practical, unfortunately ... Mrs Woolley, incidentally, would not recognise our use of the word 'vegetable'; in the English of the time there were roots, like parsnips and carrots, and greenstuffs of herbs, which effectively meant the green leafy part of a plant. Thus it is that lettuce and spinach are referred to as 'herbs' along with parsley, thyme and the like.

This first recipe shows, perhaps, that fennel was an unusual vegetable, simply because Mrs Woolley thought people might need advice on cooking it, even in the simplest manner. Commoner vegetables are generally treated more elaborately. She also gives precise directions for picking it: 'Cut your fennel when it is still young, and about four fingers high.'

Fennel
To make a Sallet of Fennel

The original title is an example of the loose way people referred to almost any vegetable dish as a 'salad'. I was mildly surprised to find a recipe for fennel in Mrs Woolley's writings; she must have been among the first people to cook it in England, as it only seems to have arrived from Italy after the Restoration and has only recently become at all common in this country. Even now, it is usually imported. Obviously it was a delicacy, as Mrs Woolley treats it almost like asparagus.

2–3 heads of fennel, halved lengthways	*Salt and pepper* *2oz/50g butter*

Cook the fennel in boiling salted water until just tender. If you like, you can tie them in bundles to make them stay upright, as Mrs Woolley recommends, which ensures that the narrow tops don't overcook while the base is underdone. When they are done, drain them thoroughly. Return them to the pan and toss them up with the butter, salt and pepper. It is worth trying a variation, not mentioned in the original recipe but referred to elsewhere – 'drawn butter'. This is simply melted butter mixed over a low heat with a little vinegar or wine, which gives the sauce an extra tang.
Serves 4.

Like the last, this next one shows that, when fresh vegetables were available, contemporary cooks treated them well and simply.

Green Beans
To fry Garden-beans

I'm not quite sure which kind of bean Mrs Woolley meant by 'garden beans', but presumably they were of the same type as modern French or string beans. The cooking method is similar to petit pois *à la Français*, with parsley replacing the mint.

> *1lb/450g green beans*
> *Small bunch (12) spring*
> *onions, cleaned and roughly*
> *chopped*
>
> *2oz/50g butter*
> *1 tablespoon fresh chopped*
> *parsley*

> *Boil the beans and onions in salted water for 10–12 minutes. When the beans are just ready, drain them well. Return the pan to a low heat, add the butter and parsley, and heat through gently until the butter has melted. Transfer to a serving dish and garnish with a sprig of parsley.*
> *Serves 4.*

Sorrel is difficult to get hold of, as most shops don't find it worth their while to sell it. Undoubtedly it is something of an acquired taste, but as it is very easy to grow, those who enjoy it shouldn't have to go without.

Sorrel
To make a Sorrel-Sallet

Once again, Mrs Woolley calls this a 'Sallet', where a modern cook would probably not because it is served hot, and nowadays salads are deemed to be cold. Certainly, seventeenth-century people did not share the blinkered view of some of their descendants, who, faced with a choice of eight salads in the English restaurant where I once worked, would say: 'I'll just have salad', meaning, of course, lettuce and nothing else. This recipe makes enough for four people as a first course, but it can also be served as a condiment, in which case omit the eggs and use only half or a quarter of the given quantities.

2lb/900g sorrel	2 teaspoons muscovado sugar
2oz/50g butter	4 eggs
Salt and pepper	1 oz/25g raisins, boiled for
1 tablespoon vinegar	2 minutes

Wash the sorrel very thoroughly, cut off the hard stalk-ends and chop roughly. Put it into a saucepan with just the water still clinging to it, cover very tightly and cook over a low heat for about 10 minutes, stirring it occasionally.

When it has reduced almost to a purée, take it out of the pan and drain. Melt the butter over a low heat and return the sorrel to the pan. Stir well, season to taste and add the vinegar with the sugar dissolved in it. Add more butter if you like it.

Put the eggs into cold water, bring to the boil and cook for about 5–6 minutes – they should not be hard-boiled, but still soft at the yolk. Pile the buttered sorrel on to a serving dish, shell the eggs, halve them lengthways, and arrange them round the dish, with the cut side upwards. Sprinkle the raisins over the sorrel and serve.

Serves 4 (but see above)

In the seventeenth and eighteenth centuries, sweet spinach tarts were very popular; they are still found in France, but are rare in England. This is a pity: the combination of sugar and fruit with spinach is delicious and refreshingly unusual. The second of these two recipes is one of Mrs Woolley's variations on the basic theme; once you have become accustomed to the idea of sweetness and spinach, I'm sure others will occur to you.

Spinach Tart with Dried Fruit
To make a Spinage or Lettice Tart

I did try this one with lettuce, but the results were disappointing –

cooked in this way, lettuce has little or no flavour, especially when compared to spinach.

2lb/900g fresh spinach
4oz/100g stoned prunes,
   currants or raisins

4oz/100g butter
3–4 teaspoons cinnamon
4 teaspoons sugar

Wholemeal pastry to line and cover a 10in/25cm flan dish

Pre-heat the oven to Gas Mark 5/190°C/375°F.
Wash the spinach very thoroughly, remove the stalks and roughly chop. Cook, in just the water clinging to it, until tender. Then follow Mrs Woolley's advice to 'put them into a Cullender to drein the water from them till they be very dry'. Press the cooked leaves hard into a colander or sieve to squeeze out all the water.
Grease the flan dish and line with pastry. Spread half the butter over the bottom, then add a layer of fruit, reserving some of it. Next, sprinkle liberally with cinnamon and sugar, then add the spinach. Put in the rest of the ingredients in reverse order – sugar, cinnamon, fruit and butter – and cover the pie with the pastry lid, moistening the edges of the pastry with milk.
Make a slit in the top and bake in a moderate oven for about 30 minutes.
Serves 4–6.

Spinach Tart with Wine and Cinnamon

2lb/900g spinach
A glass of white wine
2 teaspoons rosewater

3–4 teaspoons cinnamon
4 teaspoons sugar

Wholemeal pastry to line and cover a 10in/25cm flan dish

Preheat the oven to Gas Mark 5/190°C/375°F.
Prepare the spinach as before, cook with the wine until tender, and drain thoroughly. Return to the pan, add the remaining ingredients and, in Mrs Woolley's words, 'boyl it till it be as thick as Marmalade', ie for 4–5 minutes, until it forms a thick purée. Fill the tart and bake in a moderate oven for about 30 minutes.
Serves 4–6.

Ideally, the next tart should be made with sorrel, and I've emphasized this in the title. However, this is simply because I think the combination of flavours is so good, and not for strict historical reasons. Mrs Woolley uses a lot of sorrel in her recipes, and I think it's perfect here, if you can get it.

Sorrel and Apple Tart
A Fryday-Pye without Fish or Flesh

The original name is a reminder that in the seventeenth century, many religious obligations, including the meatless Friday, were still respected. For the filling Mrs Woolley actually specifies 'green Beets', presumably the same as beet greens, which are rather dull eating. If you have to eat them, this recipe cheers them up immensely. Spring or winter greens can be used too, but sorrel, if you can find it, is the best as its sharp flavour contrasts well with the apple. Spinach is easier to find, and makes a good substitute.

2lb/900g sorrel or spinach
2oz/50g currants
½in/1cm piece of fresh
  ginger, grated, or 2
  teaspoons dried ginger

2 eating apples, peeled, cored
  and grated
2oz/50g butter
2 dessertspoons soft brown
  sugar

Wholemeal pastry to line and cover a 10in/25cm flan dish

Preheat the oven to Gas Mark 5/190°C/375°F.

Wash the sorrel or spinach – 'in several waters', in the old phrase – and cut out the stalks. Cook for a minute or two over a moderate heat until it has darkened and reduced to a pulp. Drain very thoroughly, then mix it well with the grated apple, currants and ginger.

Line the flan dish with half the pastry, and spread butter over the bottom. Sprinkle some sugar on the butter, then fill the tart with the sorrel mixture, add some more butter and sugar to taste, and close up. Make two slits in the top and bake for about 30 minutes.

If you use spinach, try adding a little lemon juice; if you use sorrel, there's no need, as the potash in its leaves gives it plenty of sharpness.

Serves 4–6.

In the seventeenth century, sweet potatoes were simply known as 'potatoes', because the sweet potato arrived from the New World first. By the end of the eighteenth century, however, the 'Virginia' or 'Bastard' potato had relegated the 'Spanish' or 'sweet' potato to the fringes of the table. The sweet potato was regarded in Shakespeare's time as an aphrodisiac; I can promise nothing, but the following recipes strike me as being warmer and more inviting than oysters, at any rate.

Sweet Potatoes Fried with Butter and Vinegar
To fry Potatoes

Mrs Woolley says of sweet potatoes, and also Jerusalem artichokes, prepared in much the same way, that 'these for a need may serve for Second-Course Dishes'. I think that they are excellent with strongly flavoured roast meat, especially game such as venison, or simply on their own, as a form of pure indulgence.

1½lb/675g sweet potatoes	*2oz/50g butter*
1 tablespoon cider vinegar	*2 teaspoons raw cane sugar (or*
1 dessertspoon rosewater	*to taste)*

Gently scrub the potatoes, and boil them whole in salted water for about 15–20 minutes, or until tender. Drain them thoroughly and cut into ½in/1cm slices.

Melt the butter in a frying pan and add the rosewater, vinegar and sugar. Stir briefly, then put in the potatoes and cook gently on both sides for 3–4 minutes, making sure they soak up the buttery liquid. (Like 'common' potatoes, they are improved by association with lavish amounts of butter, an unhealthy fact of life for which Nature must be held to blame.)

Serve hot, with any remaining liquid dribbled over them.
Serves 4.

It's worth noting that in the next recipe, Mrs Woolley once again gives a dish which, at a pinch, could be served either as a sweet or a savoury course. Sweet potatoes, with their natural sweetness and richness of flavour, must have suited the seventeenth century perfectly.

Sweet Potato Pie
To make a Potato Pye

This is a substantial dish of spicy sweet potatoes which can accompany a stew, or be served as a separate course. This recipe should be enough for four people as an accompaniment.

1lb/450g sweet potatoes	*4 fl oz/125ml medium-dry*
4oz/100g butter	*white wine*
½ teaspoon ground mace	*1 egg, beaten*
2 teaspoons cinnamon	*Shortcrust pastry to cover a*
1 teaspoon dark raw cane	*7in/18cm pie dish*
sugar	

Preheat the oven to Gas Mark 5/190°C/375°F.

Scrub the potatoes and boil them in lightly salted water for about 15 minutes, depending on size – they should be tender but not too soft. Drain and cut into ¼in/5mm slices.

Grease the pie dish with a third of the butter, then cover the bottom of it with a layer of potatoes. Sprinkle on some of the spice, add some more butter, then another layer of potatoes. Continue until you have used up all the spice and potatoes, then melt the remaining butter and beat it together with the egg, wine and sugar. Pour the mixture over the pie filling.

Cover with the pastry, make two slits in it, and bake for about 20–25 minutes. The amounts of spices, and more especially butter, should be taken as a minimum; sweet potatoes always benefit from plenty of both. Indeed, this is perhaps a good place to emphasize the fact that most of the dishes in this book which contain butter and/or spices will not be harmed by a generous hand in the addition of either.

Serves 4.

Salads in the seventeenth century were often designed as much for show as for eating, but Mrs Woolley's recipes are very definitely not just decorative. These two examples give an idea of her winter recipes, when fresh green vegetables were unavailable.

A Winter Salad
A Grand Sallet

I've said that Mrs Woolley was not interested in purely 'designer' salads, but even so, she knew the value of presentation. The ingredients of this one are arranged round a 'wax tree set in the middle of the Dish', and in turn the other dishes on the table would have been arranged round the salad. If you haven't got a wax tree, an idea from another of Mrs Woolley's recipes is quite fun: stick one or two tall sprigs of fresh rosemary into half a boiled egg, and use that as your centrepiece. I've substituted fresh green beans for the original's pickled beans, and I've also decided to omit Mrs Woolley's throwaway suggestion that one might add 'the Flesh of a Roasted Hen, with Sturgeon, and Shrimps', as being a little extravagant, though of course, one can add any of those ingredients if desired.

4oz/100g raisins	*2 turnips, peeled*
4oz/100g almonds	*4oz/100g cucumber or*
4oz/100g olives	* gherkins*
4oz/100g capers	*1 lemon*
8oz/225g French beans	

Cook the beans in salted boiling water for about 8–10 minutes, or until they are just al dente, and drain. Do the same with the turnips, then cut them into matchsticks – the original instruction is to cut them 'in several Figures', that is, fancy shapes. Cut the cucumbers into large dice, or if using gherkins, cut them in half, and cut the lemon into eight wedges.

Arrange all the different ingredients round the dish in whatever elegant pattern appeals to you – it can be made to look very attractive. Garnish the edge of the dish with the lemon, and serve as part of a first course. I have already mentioned a salad that was decorated with the buds of fresh herbs, and a more modest variation on that idea can be employed here. If you grow chives, cut some of the stalks when they are in flower and add them to the garnish round the edge of the serving plate – they look and smell wonderful.

Serves 4–6.

The next recipe is one of the most straightforward in all Mrs Woolley's books, and must have made a refreshingly simple change on a table full of elaborate dishes, especially in contrast to other, more complicated arrangements of salads.

Vegetable Vinaigrette
A Good Cold Salad of Several Things

This is Mrs Woolley's original title for a dish that may well have helped to use up leftover vegetables. I think it could be related to the basic 'English boiled salad', which can, in fact, be rather more appetising than it sounds. The essential thing is not to overcook the vegetables, but to keep them *al dente* and full of their natural flavour, rather than soft, soggy and tasteless.

1 small cauliflower   *Olive oil*
1 bunch of new carrots   *Wine vinegar*
8oz/225g baby turnips   *Salt and pepper*
8oz/225g parsnips

Divide the cauliflower into florets, and cut the roots into strips about 2in/5cm long. If you like, you can emulate contemporary practice and cut the vegetables into interesting shapes or 'figures' to make them more decorative. (Imogen, in Shakespeare's Cymbeline, *'cuts our roots in characters').*

Lightly boil the vegetables in a little salted water, or better still, steam them, until they are tender but still quite crisp. Drain them very thoroughly and allow to cool.

Arrange on a serving plate, and make up a simple vinaigrette dressing, which can either be poured over the roots, or served separately as a dip. This makes a good winter hors d'oeuvre for a dinner party.

Serves 4–6.

Mushrooms are not strictly vegetables, but this chapter seemed the best place to put a couple of Mrs Woolley's recipes for them. Although she describes some mouthwatering dishes, it is often difficult to guess the fact from the names she gives them which sometimes seem to be almost perversely unappetising. The two mushroom recipes given here are good examples: 'stewed or fried' sound like a caricature of traditional English cooking practices, but the results are imaginative and delicious.

Marinated Poached Mushrooms
Mushrooms Stewed

On Mrs Woolley's dinner table, these mushrooms would have been served up like many other things, in one large dish, from which everyone would have taken what they wanted (and sometimes, presumably, what other people wanted as well). However, they can be served very elegantly in individual dishes, and make a very good light first course. The dish is much improved if it is made with proper wild mushrooms with plenty of flavour – the cultivated ones can be a bit too bland and well-bred.

1½lb/675g mushrooms, wiped	2oz/50g butter
½ pint/300ml medium-dry white wine	1 tablespoon fresh chopped thyme
1 medium onion, peeled and quartered	Pinch of salt
6 peppercorns, bruised	½ teaspoon freshly grated nutmeg
1 orange, in segments	Juice of a lemon

Wipe the mushrooms – don't peel them, as this reduces the flavour – cut off the hard ends of the mushroom stalks and halve or quarter the larger ones. Marinate them in the wine for about half an hour.

Drain the mushrooms, and cook in a tightly closed pan over a low heat for 5–10 minutes. Drain off the liquid they will have produced, add the onion, peppercorns, orange, butter, thyme and salt, and cook for a further 15 minutes or until as tender as desired. If you feel they need any more liquid while cooking, add some of the wine used for marinating.

Then take out the mushrooms, along with some of the onion and orange pieces, transfer to preheated ramekins, sprinkle with the nutmeg and lemon juice, and serve.

Serves 4.

The second mushroom recipe also involves oranges, but in other respects it is a much more complicated dish, though well worth the extra trouble.

Fried Mushrooms with Claret and Orange Sauce
Mushrooms Fried

The long list of ingredients and elaborate preparation indicate the amount of trouble Mrs Woolley thought it worth giving to mushrooms, which in her time would all have been wild and hence fuller of flavour than the cultivated variety generally available today. (Anyone who has picked fresh field mushrooms and eaten them fried in butter for breakfast will know what I mean.) However, even the blandest, palest products of scientific cultivation will be transformed by this heady concoction of flavours.

1½lb/675g mushrooms
¾pt/450ml water
¼pt/150ml red wine vinegar
2 sprigs each of fresh thyme,
  marjoram and rosemary or
  1 teaspoon each dried

2 bay leaves
2 blades mace
3 cloves
3 cloves of garlic, peeled
Salt
1oz/25g butter

For the sauce:
¼pt/150ml claret
Juice of 2 oranges
2oz/50g butter
2 teaspoons creamed
  horseradish
1 orange and 1 lemon,
  quartered

1 teaspoon freshly ground
  nutmeg
Salt and pepper
2 egg yolks
1 clove of garlic, peeled

Wipe the mushrooms carefully, remove the hard ends of the stalks, and halve or quarter any large ones. Put the water, vinegar, herbs, spices, garlic and salt into a saucepan and bring to the boil. Add the mushrooms, reduce the heat and simmer, covered, for about 25 minutes, or until the mushrooms are quite soft. (Don't let them get too flabby, though.)

Take them out and drain them thoroughly – if necessary, dry them on kitchen paper. Melt the butter in a frying pan and gently fry the mushrooms for about 5–6 minutes – 'till they be brown'.

To make the sauce, melt the butter in a saucepan and add the claret, orange juice, horseradish and nutmeg. Bring to the boil, then lower the heat slightly and cook for 8–10 minutes.

Meanwhile, beat the eggs lightly in a bowl and rub a serving dish all over with the cut clove of garlic.

Allow the liquid to cool for a minute, then pour a little into the beaten eggs and mix well. Pour this liaison back into the saucepan and re-heat, stirring constantly, until the sauce has thickened. Adjust the seasoning. Arrange the mushrooms in the serving dish, pour round the sauce and serve 'garnisht with Oranges and Lemons'.

Serves 4.

So many of Mrs Woolley's recipes involve eggs in one form or another that it seemed superfluous to have a section of egg dishes. Most of the egg dishes are in the puddings chapter, but she includes some dishes whose main ingredient is egg, and which are more savoury than sweet. Here's one of them, a kind of *de luxe* coddled egg.

Buttered Eggs with Herbs
A Made Dish for Fish-Dayes

A 'made dish' was a general term for anything not obviously roast or boiled or stewed: a dish where, perhaps, one couldn't immediately tell what the ingredients were. Its direct descendant is the 'made-up dish', probably foreign, of which all decent (ie insular) English people were, or are, supposed to be deeply suspicious. Made dishes were a useful standby for meatless days, when the usual array of meat pies, joints and puddings were not permitted. This particular dish is most easily made in one of those pans designed for producing perfect 'poached' eggs, which are in fact buttered, or coddled, eggs. Allow 1–2 eggs per person, depending on their size (the eggs' size, that is).

4–6 eggs	*1 teaspoon sugar*
1 dessertspoon each of freshly	*1 teaspoon dried ginger*
chopped sage, thyme and	*1 teaspoon cinnamon*
marjoram, or 1 teaspoon	*½ teaspoon ground mace*
each dried	*2oz/50g butter*
Pinch of salt	*4 slices of wholemeal toast*

Beat the eggs in a jug with the herbs, salt, sugar and spices. Fill the egg poacher with water, put a dab of butter in each dish and heat until the butter has melted and the water is just boiling.

Pour some of the mixture into each dish, put on the lid and cook for about 10 minutes, until the eggs have gone quite hard – similar to a Spanish omelette. Mrs Woolley says 'till it be hard enough to slice'. Turn them out on to the buttered toast and serve immediately.

They make an interesting variation on the breakfast egg, if you still have enough time and few enough doctors to allow you that pleasantly old-fashioned institution, or they can be served as a light lunch dish or first course.

Serves 4.

Finally, a recipe for soup. There are very few such recipes in Mrs Woolley's books, perhaps because she thought that anyone could make it. When they do appear, as often as not they are healing broths, usually with specific restorative purposes. Perhaps inevitably, there is a recipe among her medical prescriptions for chicken soup. This barley broth also tastes as though it might have medicinal value, and perhaps Mrs Woolley thought well of it too as she gives two versions of it.

Rich Barley Soup
To make Barley broth

One of the two recipes is a modest affair, thickened in the medieval manner, which Mrs Woolley often uses, with breadcrumbs. The other, which I have adapted, is more luxurious, thickened with egg yolks and given added bite by the addition of a little sack, or sherry. Both are based on a rich stock made from a knuckle of veal; if this isn't available, use a good home-made beef or chicken stock instead.

╭───╮

*2pt/900ml beef or chicken
  stock*
4oz/100g pot barley, washed
*A good handful of fresh
  thyme, parsley and sage,
  roughly chopped, or 2
  teaspoons each dried*
Salt
3 dates, chopped

2oz/50g raisins
2oz/50g currants
2oz/50g butter
1 egg yolk
*1 tablespoon medium-dry
  sherry*
*1 dessertspoon rosewater
  (optional)*

Put the stock, barley, herbs and a pinch of salt into a saucepan and boil for about 30 minutes. Add the dried fruit and cook, on a lower heat, for another 30 minutes. Cut the butter into small pieces and stir it into the broth, and let it simmer for another 10 minutes.

Beat the egg yolk lightly with the sherry, and add a spoonful of the hot broth to this mixture. Return it to the pan and stir it in well. Add the rosewater, if desired – this will give the broth more of a sweet flavour – and serve.

This is a good, substantial soup, and with plenty of wholemeal bread, it will make a good lunch on its own. If there's any left over, a good way to finish it is to drive off the liquid by reheating it, stir in some more butter, and serve it as a vegetable, a little like a de luxe version of the Russian kasha, or buckwheat with butter.

Serves 4.

PUDDINGS AND SILLABUBS

IT is perhaps a mistake to use the word 'puddings' for the title of this chapter. In the seventeenth century and long after, a pudding was a specific dish, sweet or savoury, usually made with a suet crust and steamed or boiled (like steak-and-kidney pudding), rather than another word for dessert, sweet, or afters. If we want a standard name for the sweet course at the end of the meal, dessert probably has historical claims, describing the fruits, nuts, and other dainties eaten after the meal proper had been cleared away and the cloth drawn to reveal the host's fine mahogany table-top. It's a seventeenth-century coinage, from French *desservir*, to clear a table. (The name still holds in some Oxford colleges, where after dinner at High Table, the dons and their guests retire to the common room for fruit, nuts and wine.)

Regardless of their generic title, sweet dishes were very popular in the seventeenth century. Perhaps part of the reason for this was that sugar was one of the few foodstuffs to fall in price during the period, from about 1/6d (7½p) down to 6d (2½p) per pound at the end of the century. One of its major uses was in preserving fruit; there are dozens of recipes for preserving in all the cookery books of the time. In view of the widespread use of sugar, it's intriguing that one of Mrs Woolley's hints is a way of making sweet cakes *without* using sugar:

> *Take Parsneps, and scrape or wash them clean, slice them thin, and dry them well, beat them to powder, mixing one third part thereof with two thirds of fine Wheatflower; make up your Paste into Cakes, and you will find them very sweet and delicate.*

This anticipates the commercial extraction of sugar from sugar beet by about 250 years. However, the general appetite for sugar in all dishes, even sprinkled on boiled plaice in one recipe, was too great to be satisfied with parsnip-based substitutes.

A healthier ingredient in many tarts, pies and other puddings was of course fruit, ranging from a variety of apples and pears (another choice which we have lost, by and large) to expensive imported oranges. These latter retailed at prices up to a shilling (5p) each – as much as an average manual labourer might earn in a day. It was not just imported fruit that was expensive; one could pay 5/4d (27p) for eight pounds of English cherries. However, despite this wide range, apples seem to have been the stape fruit for cooking, as is shown by the number of apple recipes included here.

Eggs, cream, butter and spices all play prominent parts in the following recipes, but their presence in savoury dishes, too, reminds us that cooks made far less distinction between 'sweet' and 'savoury' than we do. The spinach tarts in the vegetable section are quite sweet, as is the sweet potato pie. Either could be served as, or with, a main course, or even as a dessert – though of course, the seventeenth-century understanding of 'main courses' and so on was different from ours. Perhaps we tend to classify flavours according to where they come in the long-standing pattern of the meal, as much as by their objective taste. This selection of desserts starts with some traditional English 'afters' (another example, by the way, of a course being defined not by its flavour but its position in the menu), fruit pies and tarts.

Apple Tart
To make a Pippin-Tart

This is a closed tart made with small eating apples. Mrs Woolley's instructions are very precise, by her standards:

> *Take of the fairest Pippins, and pare them and then divide them just in halves, and take out the cores clean; then roul the Coffin flat, and raise off a small Verge, of an Inch or more high; lay the Pippins with the hollow side down-ward, close one to another, then put in a few Cloves, a stick of Cinnamon broken, and a little piece of Butter; cover all clean over with Sugar, and so cover the Coffin, and bake it as other Tarts ...*

The 'coffin' was the pastry case for any tart or pie; although it may sound strange to modern ears, it has no direct connection with the funereal container except for a shared descent from an old French word for a basket. I use an ordinary pie dish to make my coffin – it is quite possible that Mrs Woolley's pastry was a hot-water paste which would stand upon its own, even to a height of 'an Inch or more', without a dish to support it. In adapting the recipe I've used an enriched shortcrust, which is probably more to modern tastes. Her final instruction is to mix butter and rosewater, and 'anoint the Lid all over with it, then scrape or strew on it a good store of sugar':

the scraping and strewing depending on whether the cook used loaf sugar or the ready-ground variety. The end result is very impressive, and tastes delicious especially when accompanied by cream.

For the pastry:
8oz/225g flour   *1 egg yolk*
5oz/150g butter   *water*

For the filling:
1lb/450g small eating apples,   *2 teaspoons cinnamon*
*   peeled, cored and halved*   *1 dessertspoon dark*
2oz/50g butter   *   muscovado sugar*
1 dessertspoon rosewater   *1 dessertspoon golden*
3 cloves   *   granulated sugar*

Preheat the oven to Gas Mark 5/190°C/375°F.

Make the pastry in the usual way, but using the egg yolk, lightly beaten with 1 tablespoon water, for liquid. This gives the pastry a richer texture and finer colour. Reserve just under half for the lid, and roll the rest out (not too thinly), and line a tart case with it.

Put the apple halves cut-side downwards in the tart, packing them close together so that they cover the base. If you can't get apples all the same size, cut the larger ones to fit. Sprinkle them well with the cinnamon, and add the cloves, lightly bruised. Cut half the butter into pea-sized pieces and dot around the fruit, and finally sprinkle on the muscovado sugar.

Roll out the remaining pastry for the lid and cover the tart, moistening the edges of the pastry with a little milk to seal it. Make two small slits in the stop of the tart and bake for about 25–30 minutes, or until the pastry is well coloured.

Meanwhile, melt the remaining butter with the rosewater in a small pan. When the tart is ready, take it out of the oven and, using a pastry brush, 'anoint the Lid' with the butter and rosewater mixture. Sprinkle on the golden granulated sugar and return the tart to the oven for another 5–6 minutes, until the sugar has hardened. Serve hot or cold.

Serves 4–6.

Such is the modern apathy towards the old variety of orchard fruit that I can label both the last recipe and the next as 'apple' tarts, when in Mrs Woolley's time they were pippin and codling tart respectively. No doubt the different apples were deliberately chosen to suit different dishes, and the distinction between them, which we can no longer fully recapture, had an important effect on the flavours.

Apple Tart baked with Custard
To make a Codling Tart

A codling is, or was, a type of cooking apple, and in this recipe it is combined with a rich custard, which may have been a regional speciality. The traveller Celia Fiennes tracked this dish down in St Austell, Cornwall, in 1698:

> my Landlady brought me one of the West Country tarts, this was the first I had met with, though I had asked for them in many places in Sommerset and Devonshire, its an apple pye with a custard all on the top, its the most acceptable entertainment that could be made me.

This being Cornwall, the custard was made with 'clouted cream', no doubt making it even more acceptable. Eating apples can be used in place of cookers, in which case less sugar will be needed. Mrs Woolley's recipe for 'a very fine Custard', which is ideal for this tart, is given below, and can be served separately as an accompaniment to fruit or 'French comfits', ie sugar-coated nuts, etc.

2 large Bramleys or other cookers, peeled, cored and chopped

1 teaspoon rosewater
2 teaspoons raw cane sugar
1 teaspoon cinnamon

For the custard:
6 fl oz/180ml double (thick) cream
2 eggs
1 egg white (optional)
1 in/2.5 cm cinnamon stick

A pinch of freshly grated nutmeg
2 teaspoons light muscovado sugar
Shortcrust pastry

Preheat the oven to Gas Mark 5/190°C/375°F.
Stew the apples, sugar, rosewater and spice in a covered pan over a low heat until it has all reduced to a thick purée.
Meanwhile roll out the pastry and line a greased 7in/17cm tart dish with it. When the apple mixture is ready, allow it to cool for a few minutes, then fill the pastry case and bake in the

centre of the oven on a metal baking sheet for 25–30 minutes, until the pastry is almost done.

To make up the custard, heat the cream with the spices until it is just bubbling, and let it cook over the lowest possible heat for a few minutes. Beat the eggs lightly – if you use the extra egg white, the finished dish rises slightly more and looks very impressive. Take the cream off the heat, remove the cinnamon stick and allow to cool for a minute or two, then stir a tablespoon of it into the beaten eggs and mix well. Mix this liaison back into the cream and sweeten to taste.

Take the tart from the oven and pour in the custard. Return to the oven and continue baking on a slightly lower heat until it has just set, and turned a deep golden yellow colour. It looks and tastes equally attractive served hot or cold.

Serves 4–6.

Apples were not the only fruit easily available to the country cook; the orchard might also yield damsons, which, incidentally, owe their name to Damascus, the oldest city in the world.

Damson Tarts
To make a Damson-Tart

As her title shows, Mrs Woolley gives a recipe for one large tart, and indeed this does look very impressive. However, I prefer to make a lot of little tarts, which are just as delicious but seem somehow to go further, while not inducing the same feeling of guilt. The original recipe is very simple and lucid:

> Take Damsons and seeth them in Wine, and strain them in a little Cream, then boyl your stuff over the fire, till it be thick, and put thereto Sugar, Cinnamon and Ginger, but set it not in the Oven after, but let your Paste be baked before.

Mrs Woolley doesn't mention stoning the damsons first, but I think this is essential, unless you want to amuse yourself watching guests trying to dispose of the stones discreetly. I've made these tarts with an ordinary shortcrust, but they are especially delicious made with *pâte sucrée*. Although pastry had developed quite a lot from the flour and water crust of the Middle Ages, using the *pâte sucrée* is probably *not* authentic. The combination of the rich filling and the melting pastry is, however, irresistible. The following ingredients make about a dozen small tarts.

For the pastry:

4oz/100g flour	*Pinch of salt*
2 egg yolks	*2oz/50g butter*
2oz/50g golden granulated sugar	

For the filling:

1lb/450g damsons	*10fl oz/300ml red wine*
1 tablespoon dark muscovado sugar	*2 teaspoons ginger*
	2 teaspoons cinnamon
1 tablespoon double cream	

Preheat the oven to Gas Mark 5/190°C/375°F.

First, halve and stone the damsons, and marinade them in the wine for 30 minutes or longer. To make the pâte sucrée, sift the flour and salt on to a board, make a well in the centre and put in the egg yolks, butter and sugar. Work them together with the fingertips, and then gradually mix in the flour. Next, having cleaned your fingers (this is a messy business), smooth out the pastry on the board with the heel of the hand until it binds together. Don't overwork it; as soon as the pastry is a homogenous mass, form it into a ball, wrap in clingfilm and set aside in a cool place (the fridge will do) for 30 minutes at least.

Meanwhile, make the filling. Drain the marinaded damsons thoroughly, put them in a saucepan and bring to the boil. Let them boil briskly for 2 or 3 minutes, then lower the heat and add the sugar, cream and spices. Cook on a gentle heat until the damsons have turned to a purée and the mixture has reduced slightly. Leave to cool.

While the mixture is cooling, roll out the pastry and cut out about a dozen circles. Line a greased jam-tart tin with them and bake blind for 7 minutes. Let them cool, then arrange them on a serving plate and put a little of the damson mixture into each tart. They can be served hot, warm or cold, with or without cream, but I like the rich, tangy flavour better on its own.

Serves 4–6.

Another popular orchard fruit was the pear, used here to good effect in a pie.

Pear Pie
To make a Warden or Pear Pie

The original name of this recipe shows that even different types of pears were available to Mrs Woolley, wardens being crisp and for cooking. Nowadays there seems to be less choice available – I've used Conference pears, but usually it is a question of cooking what one can find. In this recipe, the pears are pre-cooked in the oven rather than being stewed – this saves them from losing their shape and becoming watery.

1lb/450g Conference pears	*2 teaspoons cinnamon*
2 tablespoons water	*2 cloves*
2 teaspoons sugar	*Pastry to line and cover a*
Beaten egg for glazing	*7in/17cm flan dish*

Preheat the oven to Gas Mark 6/200°C/400°F.

Wash the pears (don't peel them) and put them in a small casserole dish with the water and half the sugar. Cover tightly and bake in a moderate oven for about 20 minutes.

Take them out, drain and leave to cool while you make the pastry. Grease a 7in/17cm flan dish and line it with about two-thirds of the pastry.

Slice the pears lengthways and fill the tart, packing the slices closely in layers. Sprinkle the fruit liberally with cinnamon and the remaining sugar, and add the cloves. Roll out the remaining pastry to form a lid, and cover the tart. Decorate with pastry leaves, make two small cuts, glaze with the beaten egg, and bake for about 25–30 minutes.

Serves 4.

Pineapples were definitely not a common fruit in the seventeenth century, but they certainly became fashionable hot-house fruits at around this time. The name, by the way, originally referred to pine cones, and was applied to the fruit because of its similar appearance.

Pineapple Tarts

There is a painting at Ham House by Thomas Hewart of 'King Charles II being presented with a Pineapple by Mr Rose the Royal Gardener'. Obviously the fruit was regarded as being worthy of Royal attention, and was certainly something of a novelty, and indeed a luxury, at this period. This recipe, which makes about 16 small tarts, treats the pineapple in a suitably royal manner.

For the pastry:
10oz/300g flour
2–3 tablespoons water

5oz/150g butter
1 teaspoon sugar

For the filling:
1lb/450g fresh pineapple
1 dessertspoon raw cane sugar
3 egg yolks

1 small eating, apple peeled,
*   cored and chopped*
4fl oz/120ml double (thick)
*   cream*

Preheat the oven to Gas Mark 5/190°C/375°F.
    Make the pastry by rubbing the butter into the flour, then dissolving the sugar in the water and gradually blending in enough of the liquid to bind the paste. Leave the rest, then roll the pastry on a lightly floured board and cut 14–16 circles. Line a greased jam-tart tin with them and bake blind for about 20– 25 minutes.
    To make the filling, chop the pineapple into small cubes and liquidize it with the chopped apple and the sugar, then add the egg yolks and cream and mix well. Fill each tart with some of the mixture and return to the oven for another 10 minutes. Allow to cool for a few minutes before serving – these can be eaten hot or cold.
    Serves 4–6.

Dried fruit as well as fresh was used in tarts and pies. The most obvious example is the mince pie, which even in Mrs Woolley's day already contained as much, if not more, fruit than meat. I've included two examples in the meat chapter – whether they count as sweet dishes or not is difficult to decide. Mrs Woolley also provided a vegetarian version, presumably for Lenten or Friday fare, made with eggs.

Spicy Egg and Mincemeat Pies
Egg-Mince-Pye

Unlike the usual mince pies, these pies do not contain suet, which makes them attractive to vegetarians. Mrs Woolley says: 'When baked, liquor them with Butter, white-wine, sugar'. Liquoring was the process of adding extra liquid, usually wine-based, to pies after they had been baked, through a hole cut in the top of the crust. This gives them added richness, and also helps rescue pies which have become too dry. Presumably this was often a problem, given the erratic ovens of the period (though plenty of my pies have needed rescuing as well).

2 hard-boiled eggs, peeled	*2 teaspoons cinnamon*
2oz/50g currants	*2 teaspoons caraway seeds*
2oz/50g dates	*2 teaspoons rosewater*
2 dessertspoons dark	*2oz/50g butter*
muscovado sugar	*2fl oz/60ml white wine*
Juice and grated peel of one	
lemon	

For the pastry:

6oz/175g flour	*3oz/75g butter*
	Water

Preheat the oven to Gas Mark 5/190°C/375°F.

Chop the eggs finely and mingle them thoroughly with the fruit, spices, lemon juice and peel, rosewater and half the sugar. Make up the pastry in the usual way. Reserve about a third, and line a greased jam-tart tin with the remainder. (This amount should make about 10–12 little tarts.)

Fill the pies cases with the mixture, roll out the remaining pastry and cover the pies. Make a small slit in the top of each one and bake for about 25 minutes.

Heat the remaining sugar with the butter and wine in a small saucepan, stirring until it has formed a runny sauce. When the pies are ready, pour a little of the 'liquor' into each one, and serve any left over in a jug.

Serves 4–6.

It wasn't just fruit that was used in sweet tarts; there is a whole range of them made simply with cream or cream and eggs, heavily spiced. This example is flavoured with dried fruit and sherry.

Spicy Cream Tart
To Make rare Chees-cakes

This is rather a contradictory name, as this tart doesn't contain cheese, and is certainly nothing like the modern cheesecake. However, the term 'cheese' seems to have been used to describe foods whose texture was similar to soft cheese – for example, lemon cheese for lemon curd.

1/2pt/300ml single (thin)
  cream
3 eggs
2fl oz/60ml sweet sherry
1 dessertspoon rosewater

2 dessertspoons light
  muscovado sugar
2 teaspoons mixed spice
  (cinnamon, nutmeg,
  ginger)
4oz/100g currants or raisins

For the pastry:
6oz/175g wholemeal flour
3oz/75g butter

Water

Preheat the oven to Gas Mark 5/190°C/375°F.
  Make up the pastry in the usual way and line a greased 7in/ 18cm flan case.
  Beat the eggs together with the cream and heat gently. When the mixture has thickened, take off the heat and stir in the remaining ingredients. Pour into the lined flan dish and bake for 35–40 minutes.

Another version of the same variety of tart was made with almonds, as well as spices.

Almond Tart
An Almond tart

Almonds were a very popular flavouring at this period, despite being imported from Jordan and comparatively expensive – and were used in savoury as well as sweet dishes. Mrs Woolley's original is simple and laconic, but (as so often) she fails to give quantities:

> *Strain beaten Almonds with Cream, yolks of Eggs, Sugar, Cinnamon and Ginger, boil it thick, and fill your Tart therewith.*

In this case I've had to decide on amounts myself, basing them on the example of other, more precise, recipes. Another departure from the spirit of the original is the use of a rich pastry, as I found an ordinary shortcrust was a little insipid in conjunction with the spicy filling. It's probable that Mrs Woolley would not have used such a fancy paste, as pastry-making had in her day only developed as far as shortcrust and puff pastry.

For the pastry:
6oz/175g wholemeal flour	2 teaspoons golden granulated
3oz/75g butter	sugar
Water	1 egg yolk

For the filling:
2oz/50g flaked almonds	1 tablespoon dark muscovado
4oz/100g ground almonds	sugar
1 egg yolk	2 teaspoons cinnamon
4fl oz/120ml single (thin)	2 teaspoons dried ginger
cream	1 whole egg, beaten

Preheat the oven to Gas Mark 5/190°C/375°F.

To make the pastry, sift the flour into a mixing bowl and add the butter, chopped into small pieces. Rub them well together until the mixture resembles fine breadcrumbs, then mix together the egg yolk, sugar and about a dessertspoonful of water. Make a well in the centre of the flour and butter, put in the egg mixture and gradually blend them together until a smooth paste is formed. Roll it out on a lightly floured board and use it to line a greased 7in/18cm baking dish. Cover the bottom with a sheet of greaseproof paper and some baking beans or rice and bake blind for 15 minutes.

For the filling, break up the flaked almonds slightly (the easiest way is to run a rolling pin over them a few times). Put all the ingredients except the whole egg into a saucepan and stir over a low heat until the mixture becomes a thick paste. Remove from the heat, allow to cool for a few minutes, then stir in the whole egg and mix well.

Pour into the pre-baked flan and return to the oven for a further 15 minutes.

Serves 4.

Apples again – they were a very popular fruit with Mrs Woolley. This time they are used in bite-sized pasties, which seem to have been popular with both sweet and savoury fillings (for instance, the liver pasties on page 75.) These go down well at parties as an interesting variation on the usual nibbles.

Apple Pasties
To make little Apple pasties to fry

These pasties are light, tiny and spicy – the rich, tangy filling contrasts deliciously with the puff pastry wrapper. Although Mrs Woolley recommends frying them, I cannot get this method to work with puff pastry, but it is excellent with a good wholemeal shortcrust, rolled very thin. Fry them in a very little butter, about 4–5 minutes each side, until golden brown. These are best eaten hot. If they are baked instead they can be kept and eaten cold.

1lb/450g eating apples, cored and finely chopped	*½ teaspoon dried cinnamon*
	½ teaspoon freshly ground
5fl oz/150ml red wine	*nutmeg*
1 dessertspoon muscovado sugar	*½in/1cm cube root ginger, grated*
1oz/25g currants or raisins	*A good pinch of ground cloves*
Beaten egg for glazing	*8oz/225g puff pastry, or rich shortcrust if frying*

Preheat the oven to Gas Mark 7/220°C/425°F.

Put all the ingredients except the pastry in a saucepan and stew, closely covered, over a low heat until the mixture has reduced to a purée. If it refuses to reduce properly, complete the process in an electric blender or mouli-légumes. Allow to cool.

Meanwhile, roll out the pastry until it is a very thin sheet, and cut 16–20 3in/7.5cm circles from it. Put a teaspoonful of the apple mixture in the centre of each circle, and fold the pastry over it. Paint the inner edges of the pastry with milk to seal, and press them together.

Glaze with the beaten egg to ensure an inviting golden brown finish, place on a greased baking sheet, and bake in the oven for about 15–20 minutes or until the pastry has puffed up and is golden brown. These are very good served hot with chilled whipped cream.

Serves 6.

Another filling for these miniature pasties was made from oranges, which were almost more popular in savoury dishes than in sweet. Oranges were obviously served as part of the fruit course at the end of the meal, but this next recipe is the only one I've found for a 'made dish' using them.

Orange Cream Pasties
To make the Orenge Pudding

Mrs Woolley's original recipe has a balance of ingredients which is illustrative of the seventeenth century's sweet tooth:

> *Take the rind of a small Orange, pared very thin and boiled in several waters till it be very tender, then beat it fine in a morter, then put to it four ounces of fine Sugar, four ounces of fresh butter, the yolks of six Eggs, and a spoonful or two of cream.*

The resulting mixture might appeal to some people, but any flavour of oranges is completely smothered, especially as the peel is boiled. I've adjusted the amounts to bring out the tang of the fruit more. A reminder of how far kitchen technology has advanced is the way Mrs Woolley has to beat the orange peel in a 'morter'. Even such simple implements as graters had not then appeared, and they must have had an immense impact when they did.

Finely grated rind of 3 oranges	*2oz/50g butter*
	2 tablespoons double cream
2oz/50g light muscovado sugar	*2 egg yolks*
	8oz/225g puff pastry

Preheat the oven to Gas Mark 5/190°C/375°F.

Cream together the butter and sugar, then mix in the orange peel, cream and egg yolks.

Roll out the pastry very thin, and cut it into 16–20 3in/8cm (approx) discs. Put a teaspoonful of the mixture on to each circle, then fold the edges together, moistening them with milk to seal them.

Arrange the pasties on a greased baking sheet and bake for about 15 minutes, or until the pastry has puffed up and turned light golden brown. They should not be allowed to get too brown, as the pastry becomes rather hard and tough.

If you have any mixture left over, don't throw it away; heat it gently and serve it as a sauce. One other tip: I sometimes find that, if I over-fill the pasties, or fail to seal them up properly, the mixture runs out on to the baking sheet and forms a crust. Don't worry – this makes the most delicious sort of orange crisps, which can be picked off the dish and eaten.

Serves 4–6.

A return to apples, this time in a creamy chilled dish ideal for hot weather.

Creamed Apples with Wine and Spices
Apple Cream

This pudding is simple to make but tastes luscious. As in the damson tart recipe, the use of red wine prevents the dish from being too sweet, while giving it a sort of tangy richness. Mrs Woolley's original specifies 'a dozen Pippins', and Cox's Orange Pippins are certainly very good for this dish. Incidentally, she also refers to 'a race of Ginger', an old word (from the French) for a root of ginger which is still sometimes used today.

6 eating apples, peeled and sliced	1 dessertspoon muscovado sugar
5fl oz/150ml red wine	1 teaspoon grated nutmeg
1in/2·5cm piece of root ginger, peeled and grated	10fl oz/300ml double (thick) cream
Grated rind of half a lemon	1oz/25g flaked almonds

Put the apples, wine, ginger, lemon peel, sugar and nutmeg in a saucepan and stew, covered, for about 20 minutes, or until the apples are reduced to a purée. Stir the mixture thoroughly, transfer to a dish and leave to cool.

Meanwhile, whip the cream until thick, and when the apple mixture is cool fold the cream into it. Sprinkle with the almonds and chill for at least one hour before serving.

(If you have any egg whites left over from one of Mrs Woolley's other recipes – which is quite likely – you can beat them until stiff and fold them into the apple cream to create a kind of apple snow. Allow 2 or 3 whites for the quantities given here.)

Serves 4.

Gooseberries feature regularly in Mrs Woolley's recipes, but more often as an ingredient in savoury dishes, such as the Pigeons with Grapes or Gooseberries on page 76, than on their own. Here is an exception, something between the apple cream given above and the more familiar gooseberry fool.

Gooseberry Custard
To make a Gooseberry Custard

The secret of this recipe is not to pulp the gooseberries or liquidize them, but to preserve some of their texture in the finished dish. This makes more satisfying eating than a smooth version.

1lb/450g gooseberries	½ nutmeg, grated
1½pt/900ml water	3 egg yolks
4oz/100g light muscovado sugar	5fl oz/150ml double (thick) cream
1 dessertspoon rosewater	

Put the gooseberries and the water into 'a skillet or preserving pan' – any decent sized saucepan will do – and bring to the boil. Lower the heat slightly and cook until quite tender. This should only take a minute or two – the gooseberries should not be reduced to a pulp. Drain them very thoroughly, then return to a

*low heat and add the sugar, rosewater and nutmeg. Cover and
simmer for 5–10 minutes.*

*Meanwhile, lightly beat the egg yolks and mix them with the
cream. Take the pan off the heat and stir in the egg and cream
mixture, then return to the heat again and continue cooking
over a low heat, stirring continuously, until the mixture has
thickened to the desired consistency.*

'When you think it is enough,' says Mrs Woolley, 'pour it into
a Dish, and when it is cold, eat it'. Which is very sensible advice.
I generally put it in the fridge for 2 or 3 hours before
serving. If you like, add a sprinkling of fresh nutmeg as a
garnish.
Serves 4.

The frequent appearance of these cream-based recipes is indicative of
how much cream was used in seventeenth-century cooking. This
may sound luxurious, but in fact today's cooks, pampered as they
are by the luxuries of refrigeration, might have found the quality of
the cream not quite up to their standards. Mrs Woolley explains, in a
chapter of advice to dairy servants, how long it could be kept for:

> *You cannot keep Cream above three days in Summer, and six days in
> Winter without prejudice . . .*

And of course this cream was unpasteurised. However, Samuel
Pepys, for one, was not put off; he had a fondness for eating snacks
of bread smeared with cream, which however is not quite as
indulgent as it sounds to modern tastes, when one considers the
quality of the butter available. Cream was undoubtedly popular,
especially in the summer, when the lush grass meant that cows
produced richer milk and thus thicker cream. Mixing fresh fruit and
fresh cream has always been a quick and simple way of making a
dessert, and this recipe is perhaps my favourite of all.

Lemon Cream
To make Lemmon Cream

This is a delicious and unforgivably wicked pudding, a blend of
richness tempered by sharpness which, perversely, always brings
back painful memories for me. The first time I made it I had only

eaten one teaspoonful when the bowl was upset, shattering on the floor and covering the kitchen in a mouthwatering but, alas, inedible mixture of lemon cream and glass splinters. It was heart-rending to have to throw it all away. I hope you have better luck.

15 fl oz/450ml double cream	*1 teaspoon orange flower*
2 lemons	*water*
1 tablespoon raw cane sugar	*4 egg yolks*

Grate one of the lemons and reserve the grated peel for decoration. Peel both the lemons, removing all the white pith, chop them roughly and liquidize with the sugar and orange flower water.

Stir the cream over a low heat until, as Mrs Woolley says, it is blood warm (test it by dipping your finger in, unhygienic but very much appropriate technology), then stir in the lemon mixture and the eggs, lightly beaten.

Keep stirring for about 5–10 minutes, until the mixture has thickened slightly, then pour into a serving dish and allow to cool. Decorate the top with the grated lemon peel, and chill in the refrigerator for at least 3 hours.

This is very good eaten with meringues and/or fresh fruit, but the connoisseur will eat it alone, straight out of the bowl, standing next to the fridge with a greedy and guilty air.

Serves 4.

The next recipe is for a hot dessert, which, although it is called a sack posset, is not a drink at all. (Two drinks will be found in a section at the end of the chapter.) It gains its name from the use of sack and eggs, both standard ingredients in the drink.

Sack Posset
To make a Sack Posset

This is another egg-and-cream dish, a baked custard flavoured with sherry and spices. In Mrs Woolley's time, sherry simply meant wine from Jerez, in Spain, which was not necessarily fortified, though today's stronger variety makes for a rich and heady dish. If you prefer a lighter (and more authentic) taste, try a montilla, which, not being fortified, gives the sherry flavour without the added alcohol. The original recipe provides another reminder of the quantities habitually dealt with in the seventeenth-century kitchen – 'take a quart of thick cream . . . take sixteen eggs', and so on.

8 fl oz/250ml double cream
2 large eggs, well beaten
½ teaspoon ground cinnamon
½ teaspoon ground ginger

3 fl oz/100ml medium-dry
sherry
1 oz light muscovado sugar (or
to taste)
A pinch of ground cloves

Heat the cream with the spices, stirring fairly often to ensure it does not curdle. Beat the eggs, heat the sherry in a separate pan, and then add it to the eggs. When the cream has been 'seething', for a few minutes, take it off the heat, stir in the egg mixture, and add the sugar.

Pour it all into the upper pan of a double boiler and cook over a moderate heat, well covered, for 35–40 minutes, or until the posset has set to the consistency of a mousse or blancmange. If you don't have a double boiler a china bowl over a pan of boiling water will do. If you butter the basin, with a bit of practice it is possible to turn the posset out on to a dish, which looks very good.

It is quite rich, and goes very well with the contrasting taste (and colour) of fresh blackberries or raspberries arranged round the base (if you've managed to turn it out) or served separately. Serves 4.

Here is another of those baked custards which, in various forms, seem to have been popular at this period.

Baked Almond Custard
To make Almond Custard

Neither the original title, nor my own, is really an accurate description of this dish. It is thickened with breadcrumbs, which gives it a rather different texture from the other egg-and-cream custard dishes. In fact, it is rather like a very moist sponge, and can be eaten cold, though it's better hot. A related dish might well be bread-and-butter pudding; the original recipe tells the reader to 'slice the bread into' the cream, which would perhaps have the same sort of effect.

½ pint/300ml single cream	*3 eggs*
4oz/100g fine wholemeal	*1 tablespoon rosewater*
breadcrumbs	*4oz/100g light muscovado*
8oz/225g ground almonds	*sugar*
	3oz/75g butter

Preheat the oven to Gas Mark 5/190°C/375°F.

Put the cream into a bowl and mix the breadcrumbs and almonds into it. Beat the eggs together with the rosewater and sugar and stir them into the mixture.

Melt the butter in a saucepan and mix it in.

Pour the mixture into a greased baking dish and bake for about 40 minutes, or until the 'custard' has risen and browned.

Serves 6.

The next recipe has another of those confusing names. Nowadays, a florentine is a sweet biscuit made with nuts or chocolate, but in the seventeenth century it seems to have been a dish of minced beef and herbs, sometimes cooked in pastry. However, the name also refers to a dish of eggs and cream, similar to the 'chees-cake' on page 113 but not baked in pastry, and also to the cheese-like texture of the sack posset above. Quite why the name should be applied to two such different dishes, or how it came to mean what it does now, I don't know.

A Sweet Florentine
To make a Florentine

Mrs Woolley mentions 'preserved Cranberries' as an optional ingredient for this recipe. They are not easy to find these days, though I've had some success extracting the berries from cranberry sauce. Alternatively, it is possible to find fresh cranberries, especially around Christmas. For those who don't like eating too much pastry, this dish is also very good baked without the puff pastry topping.

2 eggs	1 dessertspoon light
½ pint/300ml cream	muscovado sugar
1oz/25g butter	2 teaspoons grated nutmeg
2oz/50g chopped dates	Pinch of salt
1 dessertspoon rosewater	Puff pastry (optional)
2oz/50g cranberries (optional)	

Preheat the oven to Gas Mark 5/190°C/375°F. (If you're making it without the puff pastry, a lower heat can be used – Gas Mark 3/170°C/325°F.)

Beat the eggs, mix them into the cream and stir over a gentle heat. Add the butter and continue stirring until it has melted.

Remove from the heat, add all the remaining ingredients except the pastry, and transfer into a baking dish. Roll out the pastry, cover the dish with it and bake for about 35–40 minutes.

Serves 6.

The next recipe is for a 'cheese' dish which actually does contain cheese. These little loaves make an unusual dessert, with their mixture of curd cheese and sugar. Once again, the rigid distinction between savoury and sweet is blurred, but this particular combination is not so rare – it is perhaps similar to the French habit of serving bowls of *fromage blanc* with sugar.

Miniature Curd Cheese Loaves
To make Cheese loaves

The original recipe for these 'little loaves', as Mrs Woolley describes them, shows how different were the ingredients available in the seventeenth century, especially if one lived in the country:

> *Take the tender curds of new Milk Cheese, press them very well from the whey, break them as small as you can possible; then take the crumbs of a Cheat Loaf, and as much curd as bread . . .*

A 'Cheat Loaf' was the second highest quality of wheaten bread, 'manchet' being the best. No such fine distinctions seem to be made nowadays. For the 'new Milk Cheese' I've substituted ordinary curd cheese, full- or low-fat according to taste. The loaves are quite substantial, so do not worry about making lots of them as they will fill people up fairly easily.

8oz/225g curd cheese
2fl oz/30ml double cream
2 eggs, lightly beaten
8oz/225g fine wholemeal
   breadcrumbs
Pinch of salt
2oz/50g wholemeal flour

1 tablespoon rosewater
2oz/50g butter
2 teaspoons dark muscovado
   sugar
2 teaspoons freshly ground
   nutmeg

Preheat the oven to Gas Mark 4/180°C/350°F.

Mix together the cheese, cream and eggs. Add the bread-crumbs and salt and work together thoroughly. Gradually mix in the flour until a soft dough has formed.

Divide it up into 8 pieces, and make them into little loaves – the easiest way is to roll them into cylinders, then flatten them off. Put them on to a greased baking sheet and bake for about 35–40 minutes.

To make the sauce, melt the butter with the rosewater, sugar and nutmeg. When the loaves are ready – they should be golden brown and slightly risen – take them out, make a little slit in the top of each and pour on some of the sauce. Serve the remainder separately, as it goes very well with the loaves.

Serves 4–6.

Eggs were much in demand in both sweets and savoury cooking – the 'made dish for fish-dayes' on page 101 is an example of the latter. This next pudding is a type of sweet omelette.

Sweet Omelette *de luxe*
To make an Amalet

Like so many of Mrs Woolley's recipes, this is very easy to make and even easier to eat, though not perhaps for anyone worried about cholesterol. The 'amalets' could be served in place of pancakes at the end of a meal – they can be served with 'verjuice, butter and sugar' which is very similar. I have found it easier to cook the mixture in two batches, each of which will serve two people – the omelettes are very rich.

4 whole eggs and 2 egg yolks	1 lemon, quartered
4fl oz/125ml double cream	Golden granulated sugar, for
2oz/50g unsalted butter	serving

Beat the eggs well with the cream. Melt ½oz/15g butter in a small frying pan (non-stick for preference) and pour in half the egg mixture. Then, in Mrs Woolley's words, 'Stir them a little, then fry them till you find they are enough'. In other words, let the eggs cook until they become slightly firm, like an omelette – this should take about 3 or 4 minutes. Do not stir the mixture like scrambled eggs; it should form a smooth, golden-yellow mass.

To quote again from Mrs Woolley, 'a little before you put them out of the pan, turn both the sides over that they may meet in the middle, and lay it the bottome upwards in the dish'. For this to work, the 'amalet' should be fully cooked underneath, so that it will slide easily about the pan, and is still slightly runny on top.

Turn the finished amalet out on to a warm plate and repeat the process with more butter and the rest of the eggs. Melt any remaining butter and pour it over the amalets in the serving plate.

Serve with the lemon and sugar handed separately.

Serves 4.

The next recipe is another kind of sweet omelette, but made in a different, and perhaps more old-fashioned way – it's thickened with breadcrumbs, for instance. It will appeal to those who might find the previous recipe too rich: the fruit and spices in this one offset the eggs.

Apple Omelette
To make a Phrase of apples

The unusual name of this pudding may be related to 'Friar's Omelette', a similar dish from the sixteenth century. (I've also seen it spelt *froise*; which came first I don't know. Although I've called this 'phrase' an omelette, it is in fact somewhere between a pancake and an omelette. The amounts given will make enough for two big appetites, or four pickers. You may find it easier to make the 'phrases' in two batches, as if too much mixture is put into the frying pan they can turn out thick and stodgy.

2 eating apples, peeled, cored and thinly sliced	3 eggs
2oz/50g finely grated brown breadcrumbs	½ teaspoon grated nutmeg
2oz/50g butter	½ teaspoon cinnamon (optional)
1 dessertspoon rosewater	1 dessertspoon muscovado sugar (or to taste)
2oz/50g currants	

Melt the butter in a frying pan, then fry the apple slices gently until tender.

Meanwhile, beat the eggs well with the spices, dissolve the sugar in the rosewater and add to the eggs, then add the currants and enough breadcrumbs to give the mixture the consistency of pancake batter.

Pour the mixture into the pan, and spread it out over the apples. Let it cook for 2–3 minutes, then turn it over and brown the other side. Serve sprinkled with lemon juice and sugar, like a pancake.

Serves 2–4.

Pancakes nowadays are associated with Shrove Tuesday, and it is a revealing comment on how times have changed that it is probably better known as Pancake Day, its original religious significance largely having vanished. Mrs Woolley and her contemporaries, for whom the austerity of Lent was quite strict, would have regarded Shrove Tuesday as the last chance for a lavish feast, relished all the more because of their knowledge of self-denial to come. Perhaps that is why her pancakes are more special than their descendants.

Pancakes

Mrs Woolley's pancake batter is much like the type we use today, but she enlivens it with the addition of spices and a dash of white wine. If you can find it, the extra-fine wholemeal or buckwheat flour is best for making pancakes. The cooking oil is a modern interpolation, as I find I cannot get pancake batter to cook satisfactorily without it, though others may find it unnecessary.

4oz/100g plain flour	*½ pint/300ml milk to which a*
2 eggs	*tablespoon of white wine*
1 teaspoon nutmeg	*has been added*
2 teaspoons cinnamon	*A pinch of salt*
2 cloves, ground	*1 teaspoon ginger*
Butter for frying	*1 tablespoon cooking oil*

Sift the flour into a mixing bowl with the salt and spices.

Lightly beat the eggs and, making a well in the flour, put the eggs, and a little of the milk, into it. Mix together the eggs and milk, and gradually incorporate the flour. As you blend in the flour, add more milk as required.

When you have added all the liquid, add the cooking oil, beat the mixture thoroughly for 5 minutes, then leave the batter to rest for at least half an hour.

Fry the pancakes in a cast-iron pan, in as little butter as possible, over a high heat.

Serves 4–6.

SILLABUBS

Although I have read in various places that the seventeenth-century sillabub was a drink rather than a dessert, sometimes served hot, most of Mrs Woolley's recipes for the dish seem much closer to the modern variety. Indeed, I've only found one in all her works which seems to be a drink, though confusingly, she ends her recipe by telling the reader to 'eat it'. It's included in the section on Drinks. The most entertaining of her sillabub recipes is also the most impractical to make nowadays: '*Take a Pint of Verjuice in a Bowl, Milk the Cow to the Verjuice . . .*' Whether this was for a drink or a pudding is unclear, though I suppose the high-pressure jet would have been useful in creating a frothy effect. Here I have adapted three of the more 'modern' type. The first is flavoured with lemon and fresh rosemary, while the second, although more luxurious because of the added egg white, has no added flavouring in the original. It can be improved with the addition of lemon zest or orange-flower water. For greater authenticity, while retaining the sherry flavour, use the unfortified Spanish wine montilla in place of sherry.

To make a Rare Sillibub

8fl oz/240ml double cream	A few leaves of fresh
Juice and peel of half a lemon	rosemary, chopped
6fl oz/180ml white wine or	1 tablespoon light muscovado
sherry	sugar

Mix together the wine, lemon juice and sugar and stir until the sugar has dissolved.

Beat the cream in a basin with a balloon whisk or electric mixer, gradually adding the liquid, together with the lemon peel, very finely chopped, and the rosemary. When you have used up all the liquid, continue whipping if necessary until the mixture is thick enough to form soft peaks.

Transfer to a serving dish and decorate the top with any remaining lemon peel. Mrs Woolley tells us to 'set it in a cool seller, if it stand there twelve hours it will be better', but two or three hours in the fridge will do.

Serves 4.

A Whipped Sillabub

8fl oz/240ml double cream	6fl oz/180ml white wine or
1 tablespoon light muscovado	sherry
sugar	2 egg whites

Stir the sugar into the wine until it has dissoved.

Beat the cream in a basin, gradually adding the liquid. Beat until thick enough to form soft peaks, then transfer to a serving dish.

In a separate bowl whisk the egg whites until very stiff, then fold them into the cream mixture. Chill for 2 to 3 hours.

To vary the flavour, add 2 teaspoonsful of orange-flower water, or the juice of half a lemon, to the wine.

DRINKS

WITH tea and coffee too expensive for most people, and with a water supply, especially in towns, frequently polluted, the most common drinks in this period were alcoholic: beer, of varying strengths, for the majority, and wine for the upper classes. Brandy and champagne first appeared with the Restoration in the 1660s – the Earl of Bedford paid a shilling (5p) a bottle for brandy, and £6 for four dozen bottles of champagne, in 1665. Beer consumption increased with the introduction of import duty on wines, a factor which may have helped to increase the popularity of the new-fangled tea, coffee and chocolate among the well-off. Apart from these there were innumerable home-made fruit wines, including artificial claret, for which Mrs Woolley gives a recipe involving raspberry and cherry juice, cider, raisins and mustard, 'a very pleasant drink, and indeed far better and wholsomer then our common claret'. It wasn't just homebrew aficionadoes who made their own wine, though; there were sound commercial reasons too. Import duty, and the resultant expense and scarcity of French wines, led tavernkeepers to search for substitute wines; there are horror stories later in the century of vintners mixing claret with cider and even turnip juice to make it go further. Some of the home-made drinks must have been pretty powerful – take Mrs Woolley's own recipe for the innocent-sounding lemonade:

> *Take One Quart of Sack, half a pint of Brandy, half a Pint of fair Water, the Juice of two Limons, and some of the Peel, so brew them together with Sugar, and drink it.*

I haven't tried making it myself, but I imagine it could easily have caused the high jinx described on page 24.

Tea gradually fell in price, especially when the East India Company started importing it, dropping from £3 10s (£3.50) in the

1650s to about a pound in 1700. It had its enemies, who regarded it as unmanly and insufficiently nourishing, compared to beer (Cobbet was still inveighing against its pernicious effects in the nineteenth century), but it was the price which kept most people away from it. Chocolate could claim to be more nourishing, especially when eggs were added, as in the recipe below. The other recipes are for sack possets, which were the exact opposite to tea, coffee and chocolate, being traditional, national drinks made since the fifteenth century, and well suited to provide hot, satisfyingly rich drinks before cocoa came along.

Spanish Chocolate
To make the Spanish Chaculate

Mrs Woolley probably calls this 'Spanish' because cocoa beans and chocolate first came to Britain via Spain, like 'Spanish' potatoes. Twentieth-century chocolate drinkers might find this too rich a mixture, though Mrs Woolley's contemporaries probably lapped it up. If you can't face it as a drink, it makes one of the best, and simplest, chocolate sauces I've tasted. Simply halve the amount of water. For drinking purposes, you may like to use half milk and half water – the idea of making drinking chocolate with milk was current around this time, and was championed by the great physician Sir Hans Sloane. He thought chocolate good for the health, and made more easily digestible mixed with milk. It is essential to use really good plain chocolate, preferably the French *chocolat menier*, if you can find it, which is almost fifty per cent cocoa solids. (Most standard British plain chocolate is about thirty per cent, and contains vegetable fat as well as dairy fat.)

8fl oz/250ml water	*2 teaspoons dark brown cane*
4oz/100g plain chocolate	*sugar*
2–3 egg yolks, depending on size	

Heat the water and the chocolate in a saucepan until the chocolate has completely dissolved, then add sugar to taste. Let it bubble for a few minutes, then take the pan off the heat and gradually stir in the egg yolks, beaten. Return to the heat and stir until the sauce has thickened a little, and the egg yolks are cooked. Pour into mugs and drink while still piping hot. The

*amounts given don't make very much, but it is a very rich
drink; you may have to experiment with the amount of liquid to
arrive at a satisfactory result. If you are making a sauce, use half
the quantity of water and thicken to the consistency of cream.
Serve hot with ice cream, baked apples or anything that takes
your fancy.*

SACK POSSETS

A posset is usually thought of, if it is thought of at all, as a drink, a
mixture of milk, beer (or 'sack', an old word for Spanish wine) and
spices. Zabaglione is the only modern sweet I can think of which
combines eggs, sugar and alcohol, but it is not really anything like a
posset. Mrs Woolley gives three recipes for it, only one of which,
confusingly, involves milk. One of them is for a set posset, a little
like a *crème brulée*, which is in the puddings section (page 120). Of
the drinks, the first is the standard milky drink and the second a
more alcoholic version made without milk. Sherry at this period was
unfortified; a good wine to use in place of the 'sack' of the original is
montilla, which has the same sherry taste but no extra alcohol.

To make a Sack Posset

> 15 fl oz/450ml milk
> 1 teaspoon cinnamon
> 2 blades mace
> 2oz/50g ground almonds
> 1 egg yolk, beaten
>
> 2 fl oz/60ml medium white
>   wine or montilla
> 2 teaspoons rosewater
> 2 teaspoons raw cane sugar

*Bring the milk, cinnamon and mace to the boil, then stir in the
almonds and keep stirring for 2 minutes. Take the pan off the
heat and allow the milk to cool for a minute.*

*In a separate pan, gently warm the wine or sherry with the
rosewater; while it is warming, take a tablespoonful of the milk
and mix it well with the egg yolk. Return this mixture to the
milk pan, add the warmed wine mixture and stir over a low
heat.*

*Add the sugar to taste, keep stirring until it has completely
dissolved (keep the liquid hot, but don't let it boil), then pour*

*into mugs, sprinkle on a little extra cinnamon, and serve
immediately.*

A Sack Posset without Milk

8 fl oz/250ml dry sherry	*1 teaspoon cinnamon*
4 fl oz/125ml ale (any brown	*3 eggs, beaten until foamy*
ale will do; don't use	*2 oz/50g dark raw cane sugar*
ordinary bitter)	*1 teaspoon grated nutmeg*

*These quantities don't make very much; it's advisable not to
make a lot first time round as the posset is an acquired taste.*

*Bring the ale, sherry, sugar and spices to the boil together,
and keep bubbling for 10 minutes, then remove from the heat
and allow to cool for 5 minutes. Then stir in the eggs, making
sure they are thoroughly mixed.*

*Return the mixture to the pan and simmer, stirring continu-
ally, for another 5 minutes over simmering heat. A luxurious
alternative is to whisk the mixture thoroughly, which adds to its
richness. This makes quite a heady brew.*

Serves 4.

I have already discussed the various meanings of 'sillabub' in the
seventeenth century. Here is an example of the syllabub as a summer
drink, rather like a luxurious milk shake. The mixture of milk and
cream is similar to the mixture of milk and yoghurt in the Indian
lassi.

Lemon Cream Cordial
To make a Lemmon Sillibub

The flavouring of this delicious drink is a combination of fresh
lemon juice and the ubiquitous rosewater. It might be worth trying
orange-flower water as a variation, or indeed, substituting other
fruits for the lemons.

1 pint/600ml milk
½ pint/150ml single (thin)
  cream
1 dessertspoon rosewater

1 dessertspoon light
  muscovado sugar (or to
  taste)
Juice of 2 lemons

Mix the milk, cream, rosewater and lemon juice together, then add sugar to taste and stir until dissolved. Then, as Mrs Woolley says, 'Let it stand an hour, and then eat it.' This is best left in the fridge for at least an hour, preferably longer. As it's quite a rich drink, these quantities should serve 6 people, maybe more.
  Serves 6–8.

CAKES AND BISCUITS

WHEN it comes to cakes, Mrs Woolley is usually more specific in her amounts than elsewhere, and to judge by the quantities she habitually gives in her cake recipes, baking day in a large seventeenth-century household must have been quite an event. Cooks in those days made a huge variety of cakes and biscuits, and of course the average country family would have eaten home-baked bread as well. In smaller communities there would have been a communal oven at the village baker's, to which housewives could take their larger pies and cakes.

Spicy Currant Loaf
A very good Cake

The quantities Mrs Woolley gives for this recipe in *The Ladies Delight* show the sort of numbers she was expecting to feed in a reasonably large household:

> *Take to half a peck [5lb] of Flower, three pound of Currance, four Nutmeggs, four Races of Ginger, ten Cloves, four Eggs, yolkes and whites beaten well; one quart of boiled Cream, two pounds of Butter, a Porrenger full of Ale-yeast, a quarter of a pound of Sugar . . .*

The few ounces of sugar look almost out of place there, but in fact, the currants make the cake quite sweet enough. It would take an enormous tea party to munch through a cake that size, so in altering the recipes for these more abstemious times I've reduced the quantities pretty drastically. I've also made a major structural alteration by leaving out the yeast and using baking powder instead. I'm afraid yeast cookery has always been something of a sore point with me, so when I first tried this recipe I was full of (justified) trepidation. The solid dough refused to rise, perhaps because I did not use the right amount of yeast. (Mrs Woolley's 'Porrenger' of yeast didn't help much in this direction.) I fell back on an old trick, which worked. Using baking powder, or a mixture of bicarbonate of soda and cream of tartar, not only saves worry but a good deal of time, as the dough doesn't need to be left to rise.

8oz/225g fine wholemeal flour
2 heaped teaspoons baking
*   powder or 1 each of*
*   bicarbonate of soda and*
*   cream of tartar*
1 teaspoon ground cloves
2 teaspoons ground ginger

2 teaspoons ground nutmeg
4oz/100g butter
1½oz/40g golden granulated
*   sugar*
6oz/175g currants
4fl oz/125ml double cream
1 egg, beaten

Preheat the oven to Gas Mark 5/190°C/375°F.

Sift the flour with the baking powder and the spices into a mixing bowl. Cut the butter into small pieces and rub it into the flour until the mixture resembles fine breadcrumbs.

Add the sugar and the currants and 'mingle them with your Butter and Flower'.

Heat the cream until it is blood warm, and mix it with the beaten egg. Make a well in the centre of the flour and pour in the egg and cream mixture. Stir the flour into the liquid and blend them thoroughly, then shape the dough and put it into a greased 1lb/450g loaf tin.

Bake for about 45–50 minutes, then turn out on to a wire rack and allow to cool completely before serving. It should have quite a moist, sticky consistency, so don't worry if it doesn't rise very much in the oven.

As well as that 'very good Cake', Mrs Woolley gives recipes for an 'Excellent Cake' and 'fine Cakes', showing her usual high estimate for her own productions, and of course, making her book more attractive for the browser leafing through it at one of the bookstalls in St Paul's Churchyard, where many of her books were sold. Here is the recipe for 'fine Cakes'.

Rose-scented Sponge Cakes
To make fine Cakes

When I first read this recipe, I was confused by the proportion of flour to fat, and couldn't work out whether the end result was meant to be more of a sponge or a shortbread. Mrs Woolley's cavalier disregard for detail does not help settle the question:

> *Take a quart [1lb 4oz] of Flower, a pound of Sugar, a pound of Butter, with two or three yolks of Eggs, three or four spoonfuls of Rose-water, and a spoonful of yeast; then roul them out to the bigness of a Trencher, while the paste is hot, or else it will break . . .*

I tried rolling the mixture out thinly, but this was very difficult, as the consistency of the dough is more like a sponge mixture than pastry. It is easier simply to mould the paste into biscuits. The alternative was to adapt Mrs Woolley's instructions and make the paste into little cakes, which worked well. In the end I compromised, and included both methods. Another adaptation was the substitution of baking powder for yeast, for the reasons given in the last recipe. The amounts here (rather less than the original) make about 16 small cakes or biscuits.

5oz/150g plain wholemeal flour	*4oz/100g butter*
1 teaspoon baking powder	*1 small egg, beaten*
4oz/100g dark muscovado sugar	*2 teaspoons rosewater*

Preheat the oven to Gas Mark 5/190°C/375°F.

Sift the flour and baking powder into a mixing bowl. Rub the sugar through a metal sieve into the flour, or alternatively grind it in a blender to remove any lumps. Mix it thoroughly with the flour and baking powder.

Cut the butter into small pieces and add them to the bowl. Rub the butter into the flour and sugar mixture – this is the same method as for making pastry, but it is a much stickier process, because of the proportion of butter to flour.

When the ingredients are thoroughly mixed, stir in the rosewater and the beaten egg.

To bake the 'cakes', either spoon the mixture into about 16 small paper cases, and bake in the oven for 20 minutes, or shape it into biscuits, arrange them on a greased baking sheet and bake for 15 minutes. The former cook like a sponge, but harden slightly as they cool, giving an intriguing texture somewhere between biscuit and light sponge. The biscuits are crisp, and melt in the mouth – the thinner you roll them, the crisper they end up, though it's best to keep an eye on them if the paste is very thin, as they can get burned.

Serves at least 4.

For those who are worried about such things, this next recipe is probably unique among Mrs Woolley's sweet recipes in not containing any cholesterol.

Gingerbread
To make Fine Gingerbread

Mrs Woolley's 'fine Gingerbread' is nothing like its moist and spongy modern counterpart. It is quite hard and crunchy, and tastes as hot and spicy as you care to make it.

4oz/100g finely grated breadcrumbs	*2fl oz/60ml red wine*
2oz/50g soft raw cane sugar	*2 teaspoons dried ginger*
2 teaspoons cinnamon	*1 teaspoon grated liquorice stick*
½ teaspoon aniseed	

Preheat the oven to Gas Mark 4/180°C/350°F.

Mix the breadcrumbs, sugar and spices together, and dribble in the wine until you have a mushy kind of paste. Stir this over a low heat until it is quite stiff, then leave to cool for a few minutes.

Roll out the paste on a floured surface until it is quite thin, and cut into any shape you like, using old-fashioned gingerbread cutters or suchlike.

Bake them on a lightly greased sheet for about 25 minutes, depending on whether you like biscuits very slightly chewy or rock-crisp.

These gingerbreads are very good for dunking, if that appeals to you.

Jumbals or Jumbolds
To make Diet Bread or Jumbolds

In different recipes, Mrs Woolley calls these delicious biscuits jumbals, jumbolds, symbals and 'diet bread', the latter not because they are particularly low in calories (quite the reverse) but because the various flavourings in the mixture were thought to have specific digestive properties. Caraway seeds, for example, help to 'promote the urine' and dispel 'the windy colic', as Culpeper says in his *Herbal*. Whereas Mrs Woolley had servants to 'beat' her sugar fine, it would probably be easier these days to grind the sugar in a blender for a minute. It would be possible to use castor sugar, but these biscuits are not only more authentic made with unrefined sugar, they are *much* tastier. (If the mixture feels too dry, simply add a little extra rosewater.)

8oz/225g wholemeal flour	*1oz/25g ground almonds*
8oz/225g raw cane sugar	*2 teaspoons aniseed*
4oz/100g butter	*1 teaspoon coriander seeds*
1 large egg	*1 teaspoon caraway seeds*
2 teaspoons rosewater or	*1 teaspoon fresh grated*
orange-flower water	*liquorice stick*

Preheat the oven to Gas Mark 5/190°C/375°F.

Sift the flour into a mixing-bowl and thoroughly mix in the ground sugar. Cut the butter into little pieces and rub it into the mixture.

Next, make a well in the centre of the bowl, break the egg into it, add the rosewater and little by little stir the dry mixture into the liquid. When it is all well blended, sprinkle on the ground almond and spices and work them into the paste, making sure that they are evenly distributed.

Roll the paste into a soft ball and turn it out on to a floured board. It may be a little difficult, but try to roll it out quite thinly (you may need to re-flour the board several times). You can cut the paste into any shape you like with gingerbread cutters, or try the seventeenth-century method: cut the paste into strips and tie them in little knots or twist them in spirals.

Put the jumbals on a well greased baking sheet and bake for about 45–50 minutes. The longer you bake them, the crisper they become, but they are also very good while still slightly soft-centred. They tend to harden as they cool, so don't be worried if they don't seem to be very hard when they come out of the oven.

The basic recipe for macaroons has hardly changed since the seventeenth century, except that nowadays they tend not to be flavoured with rosewater, and are usually made with refined castor sugar, which tastes of nothing at all. The seventeenth-century versions are certainly more interesting.

Macaroons
Mackroons on Wafers

Mrs Woolley calls these 'mackroons'; in the seventeenth century the word was a new import and its spelling, an adaptation of the French *macaron*, had not yet settled down. It shares an ancestor with macaroni, which had arrived in the previous century from the Neapolitan *maccarone*. However, the link is only philological, and this recipe, which makes about twenty macaroons, is for the customary mixture of almonds, sugar and egg whites. It is best made with a well-flavoured sugar such as dark muscovado, finely ground in an electric blender.

2oz/50g ground almonds	*2 teaspoons rosewater*
1 dessertspoon sugar, ground	*2 egg whites*

For the wafers:

2oz/50g wholemeal flour	*2 teaspoons cinnamon*
A pinch of salt	*2 egg yolks*
1 dessertspoon sugar	*2 teaspoons rosewater*

Preheat the oven to Gas Mark 6/200°C/400°F.

To make the wafers, mix the flour, salt, sugar and cinnamon in a bowl, then make a well in the centre and add the yolks and rosewater. Gradually mix the flour into the egg yolks, working the mixture together with the fingertips, until you have a smooth, quite stiff, paste. Roll it out on a floured board and cut out about 20 1in/2cm discs. Put these on a greased baking sheet.

For the macaroon mixture, mix together the almonds, sugar and rosewater – it should form a paste. Beat the egg whites until they form stiff peaks, then mix half of the beaten mixture with the almonds and sugar. Then fold in the remaining whites – the mixture should be 'thick as Fritters', that is a thickish dropping consistency.

Drop a teaspoonful of the macaroon mixture on each wafer. Bake for about 10–15 minutes, or until slightly risen and golden brown.

Serve hot, and eat them quickly, as they tend to become a little soft after a day or so.

Serves 4–6.

INDEX